# LOOKING THROUGH
# THE WINDOW

Liam Hickey

# LOOKING THROUGH THE WINDOW

*A Picture of God's Love
for Each Day of the Year*

ST PAULS

ST PAULS
Morpeth Terrace, London SW1P 1EP, United Kingdom
Moyglare Road, Maynooth, Co. Kildare, Ireland

Copyright © ST PAULS, 1997

First published in 1997 by ST PAULS, UK-Eire

ISBN 085439 523 7

Produced in the EU
Printed by Biddles Limited Book Manufacturers

# DEDICATION

With gratitude to the people that made these stories and shaped my life:

Ferbane
St Manchan's, Lemonaghan
St. Mel's, Longford
Holy Cross College, Dublin
G.A.A. and ST PAULS, Athlone
Cherryorchard Hospital, Ballyfermot
St Paul's, Arran Quay
St Brendan's and Richmond Hospitals
Mother of Divine Grace, Raheny
St Aloysius, London
U.C.D., Belfield
Our Lady of the Wayside, Bluebell
Holy Child, Whitehall
St Brigid's, Blanchardstown
St Ciaran's, Hartstown

# FOREWORD

LOOKING THROUGH THE WINDOW gives snapshots of encouragement. The ideas for each day that touch our lives and grace our basic humanity, are prompted by the love letters we call The Gospel.

These minute thoughts a day, are grounded on the belief of God's mysterious fidelity to us, despite all our misgivings and inadequacies.

May LOOKING THROUGH THE WINDOW of the Gospel, at the landscape of our lives, brighten our hearts this day.

Liam Hickey
*1 October 1997*

# CONTENTS

# January

*1*

A New Year, a fresh start, an open page of opportunity. Mary treasures her experiences and ponders them in her heart.                    cf Lk 2,16-21

PRAYER     *Mary, you pray for us and help us to be grateful for what has been and to have the courage for what lies ahead.*

KEYWORD    *Mary.*

❧

*2*

John tells us that "God is among you but unknown to you." All humanity is baptised in the Spirit of Jesus. Only some will celebrate this Grace with the pouring of water.                    cf Jn 1,19-28

PRAYER     *Lord, we thank you that all people will see your salvation. Make us caring like you, Father, sharing like the Son and faithful like the Holy Spirit.*

KEYWORD    *Among you.*

❧

**3**    John the Baptist was to introduce Jesus
to the world's stage. But Jesus was so
ordinary that John did not recognise
him when he came.            cf Jn 1,29-34

PRAYER    *Lord, the fiddler played a haunting tune at
the street corner. All life passed by drowning
his soothing sound. He said he was 80 years
young, played the fiddle and supported his
daughter with her two children. Lord, you
find delight in your sons and daughters.*

KEYWORD    *Recognising.*

❧

**4**    The call of God's friendship comes
through Andrew and Peter. Interest in
God and religion cannot be forced, but
only invited, through the searching of
one's own heart, and the providence of
meeting others in the journey of life.

PRAYER    *Lord, faith like love is full of surprises, the
spark of God. It is a decision to take some-
one seriously, and then the heart is moved
to give generously, to think kindly, to act
justly.*

KEYWORD    *Friendship with God.*

❧

**5** In ten lines, John uses the word "see" six times. God's gift is insight, awareness of the goodness of God and his fidelity to us, his people.                    cf Jn 1,43-51

PRAYER      *Lord, help us to see your goodness in the faces of people, in the wonders of nature, in the struggle of life.*

KEYWORD    *Insight.*

❧

**6** The three "searching kings" tell us that the human heart is a lonely hunter looking for happiness. Happiness is to be found in Jesus Christ who tells us to accept one another with all our differences and oddities and our world with all its blessings, because we are God's gift.                    cf Mt 2,1-11

PRAYER      *Lord, life and this world are your gifts. Help us to grow in love with our gifts of thanks, acts of sorrow and praise.*

KEYWORD    *Searching.*

❧

**7** "You played in my team in college 40 years ago," he said. "You were a great

tryer and never gave up. You went to
London for years. You were a good man
and now you are here. You are great!
You are always welcome in my place."
Thank God. Caring and encouraging is
God's language. It is the baptism of
everyday living.                          cf Mt 3,13-17

PRAYER          *Lord, your fatal weakness is your mercy for
us. We are always your beloved, delightful
sons and daughters.*

KEYWORD         *Everyday Baptism.*

❧

**8**  Jesus called Peter, Andrew, James and
John to fellowship while they were at
their work, of mending and minding
fish nets. The call of God comes through
the ordinary, not the sensational religious experience, nor the extraordinary.
                                          cf Mk 1,14-20

PRAYER          *Lord, you hide yourself in ordinary faces,
humble places, in everyday jobs of mending
and minding, tears and joy. Help us to see
the grandeur of your providence in the
ordinary.*

KEYWORD         *Mending.*

❧

**9** A man possessed by an unclean spirit meets Jesus and it shouted at him. Jesus understands that we don't always have full control of all the influences that beset us in life.                    cf Mk 1,21-28

PRAYER    *Lord, we are loved, not because we are perfect or virtuous but because we are human. We don't always like our condition but you accept us, warts and all! In the strength of such love, help us to be loving.*

KEYWORD   *You accept us.*

❦

**10** I like the way Jesus cured Peter's mother-in-law. He took her by the hand and helped her up. There were no long prayers. Presence, touch, listening is prayer and cure.                    cf Mk 1,29-39

PRAYER    *Lord, when Pope John XXIII was worried about the conduct of the great Second Vatican Council he had just announced, one night he did not get any sleep. As he lay restless, a voice asked him, "John, who runs the Church – you or the Holy Spirit?" "All right, Lord," he said, and fell asleep.*

KEYWORD   *Not alone.*

❦

## 11

The humanity of God sees Jesus touching the untouchable and saying, "Of course I want to heal poor humanity." He gives the man a card of acceptance, to belong again to the community, to regain dignity. cf Mk 1,40-45

PRAYER *Lord, when we feel hard done by because of family situations, health, religion, education, lack of talent and opportunity, remind us of your never-changing love.*

KEYWORD *Of course I want to.*

❧

## 12

The children love this story of the paralysed man on a stretcher let down through the roof of the house by his friends in order to get near Jesus. They wouldn't give up and Jesus cured the man because of their enthusiasm. cf Mk 2,1-12

PRAYER *Lord, whatever we do, or whenever we wish to make life more livable for another human being, it registers with you and is never lost.*

KEYWORD *Enthusiasm.*

❧

*13*  It baffled the religious people that Jesus would sit and eat with sinners, before they reformed.                cf Mk 2,13-17

PRAYER  *Lord, may the peacemakers of the world be guided by your strategy to meet and eat first, and hope for reform and renewal afterwards.*

KEYWORD  *Eating with sinners.*

*14*  John seemed preoccupied with seeing, with light, with insight into the person of Jesus Christ. In his plan of salvation Jesus embraced not only people but the whole universe.                cf Jn 1, 29-34

PRAYER  *Lord, looking at the garden, one person saw the flowers, the other person saw only the weeds. Give us insight and awareness of your blessings in my life and in the lives of other people.*

KEYWORD  *Insight.*

*15*  Jesus doesn't seem impressed with fasting. God's love is about feasting. You don't fast at wedding time. You open

your mind and heart to celebrate with
the people.                        cf Mk 2,18-22

PRAYER        *Lord, self-chosen fasts are good when linked
              to giving to others, but the unchosen fasts
              that come our way are best, like living with
              others, bearing sickness, caring for family,
              worrying about money, coping with moods
              and limitations*

KEYWORD       *Fasting or feasting.*

**16**   Jesus tells how David and his followers
         ate God's Holy Bread when there was no
         other food. Jesus always invites us to
         "Take and Eat". It is we who add the
         conditions to his generosity. The Sab-
         bath is for our well-being – a gift of
         God's love, not an obligation of fear.
                                   cf Mk 2,23-28

PRAYER        *Lord, help us to see the Sabbath with new
              eyes, an opportunity to be hospitable and
              caring for others, to lend support to the
              community.*

KEYWORD       *Sabbath generosity.*

## 17

He was out of work and withered when he won a 50p treble on the horses. He said, "I am singing for the last three days," but the neighbours were critical and could not join in his happiness.

cf Mk 3,1-6

PRAYER

*Lord, help us to rejoice with those who rejoice, to be delighted for people when they plan a holiday, when they acquire a new item for the house, when they have a success in the family. May we get used to the words "I'm glad for you".*

KEYWORD

*Rejoice for others.*

## 18

When Jesus is being pressed on all sides by the crowd, he asks for the help of a boat to ease the situation.

cf Mk 3,7-12

PRAYER

*Lord, we can be so crushed by work, pain and worry of life that we lose touch even with ourselves. Help me to make time for coffee with a friend, for a visit to the store, for a hairstyle, a chat on the phone, a rest in the sun, a good book or movie, a chat with a child.*

KEYWORD

*Being crushed.*

**19** Jesus said his chosen ones were to be companions, not servants or subjects. The companion is the person one drinks coffee with, shares a drink with, eats with. There is no mention of fear, such is the Christian God.        cf Mk 3,13-19

PRAYER    *Lord, teach us how to eat and drink and share with our brothers and sisters who are different.*

KEYWORD   *Companion.*

❧

**20** Jesus goes home with a reputation. He is mobbed by the crowd. One senses the pain of Mary when the relations come to take Jesus away, convinced that he was mad.        cf Mk 3,20-21

PRAYER    *Lord, the parents agonized over the teenage party, whether to open the house to the strangers or to say no. They did not sleep much that night. Lord, bless family life with all the tensions of growth. May goodness, hospitality and kindness flourish.*

KEYWORD   *A bit mad.*

❧

**21**  They were not praying or in the chapel when the Lord called them. They were working, making and mending nets. We are all called by God to be makers and menders in our job of work in the journey of life.                    Mt 4,18-22

PRAYER  *Lord, we are makers and menders from breakfast to bedtime. Bless the work of our hands. We trust the loving providence of your hands.*

KEYWORD  *Makers and menders.*

❧

**22**  Jesus does good, but he is accused of having help from the devil. Jesus does not judge or condemn his accusers, but tells a story to try and enlighten the dark prejudiced mind, and to open the hard heart.                    cf Mk 3,22-30

PRAYER  *Lord, am I always pleased when I see others get compliments? In truth I am often begrudging in spirit. Keep me from blaming the devils. Teach me, with your help, to grow in understanding and generosity of heart.*

KEYWORD  *Begrudging devils.*

❧

## 23

We are told that Mary was outside asking for Jesus. The outside feeling suggests pain – the kind of pain parents experience when they can't reach their children fully. The feeling people have of being left out. The feeling with age that nobody understands or cares.

cf Mk 3,31-35

PRAYER     *Lord, it hurts when we feel left out, forgotten, on the outside, not understood. Help us to be grateful for what has been, and to accept what will be, with the prayers of Mary.*

KEYWORD     *Left out feeling.*

## 24

The seed never sees the golden grains of wheat. Seeds are expendable but are never lost.                         cf Mk 4,1-20

PRAYER     *Lord, your mercy and providence understands the mystery of our seed-life, with death and tragedy and disappointment, joys and sorrows, success and failure, light and darkness. Yet we are seeds that are forever precious to you. That is joy!*

KEYWORD     *Expendability is not loss.*

## 25

Jesus invites us to be light givers. We cannot rid darkness with darkness but only with light.          cf Mk 4,21-25

**PRAYER**    *Lord, I often want to repay hurt with hurt, an eye for an eye. Help me to bring your light into relationships in life, especially into the peace-making world.*

**KEYWORD**    *Only light rids darkness.*

## 26

Jesus uses stories like mirrors, inviting us to look, never forcing us. God is present to all the world in his Kingdom. His mercy is like seed; is constant but cannot be totally controlled. Nor can we judge by size; the small mustard seed seems useless, but it has a great future.
                                          cf Mk 4,26-34

**PRAYER**    *Lord, open my mind to your presence in all that exists. There is more to life than the size of accomplishments. There is YOU.*

**KEYWORD**    *Mercy, the only constant.*

**27** "Let us cross over to the other side,"
Jesus said. I thought of my crossing to
the Basket Islands in a frail boat, and
the mighty depths of the ocean gave one
a sense of great dependence.

cf Mk 4,35-41

PRAYER     *Lord, you went into the depths of humanity*
*and made the crossing. Take us with you*
*now and always.*

KEYWORD    *Crossing over.*

**28** Etty Hilsum volunteered to go with her
people to prison in Auschwitz. She died
in the concentration camp. She wrote in
her diary, "You don't ask people what
they do, you listen to what they suffer."

cf Mt 5,1-12

PRAYER     *Lord, we are poor in spirit because of our*
*weaknesses, human limitations, fears and*
*guilt. Even the rich face can hide a lonely*
*heart. We die. Thanks for blessing our*
*human condition.*

KEYWORD    *How I am or what I have.*

## 29

The young prisoner begged relief for a fix. He was chained to his habit. He was in a tomb of death, destroying himself. Using God's name, he was howling with inner conflict. He said, "Give me a prayer for help."                    cf Mk 5,1-20

PRAYER      *Lord, you were in the depths. You know the journey. Help us to be rid of chains, of darkness and destruction. Ease our inner agonies.*

KEYWORD     *Chained.*

## 30

"Lay your hands on my sick daughter", her father pleads. "If I touch the hem of his clothes I will be well", a fearful woman says. Taking the little girl by the hand, he says, "Give her something to eat". Jesus longs to touch people with healing comfort. God caresses our humanity.                          cf Mk 5,21-43

PRAYER      *Lord, help us to touch others caringly and affectionately. Bless the work of human hands and the hospitality of loving hearts.*

KEYWORD     *Affectionate touch.*

# 31

Imagine Mary today, a warm, hospitable, gracious person, feeling the pain of family rejection. Her son comes home, this ordinary, quiet young lad. Now he has a scruffy crowd hanging around him, and he has new and different ideas. He has changed.          cf Mk 6,1-6

**PRAYER**     *Lord, bless family life that has to cope with growing up with new ideas, different ways of behaviour.*

**KEYWORD**    *Change and rejection.*

# February

## 1

"Take nothing for the journey", Jesus said. Beautiful, spring scenes flash by on the train to Cork. Distant hills, trees, sheep grazing, horses standing still, clouds of coloured light, an old castle, a church spire, a cemetery, a little river, soothing greens everywhere, a football field, a racing track, a golf course, people's faces and they were all free.

cf Mk 6,7-13

PRAYER

*Lord, how I am is more important than what I have. Help me to see your gifts as loans and blessings, not possessions.*

KEYWORD

*All for free.*

## 2

Mary presents her child to God. Simeon and Anna join the celebration. Our baptisms are welcome celebrations. We all touch the baby with goodwill messages.

cf Lk 2,22-40

PRAYER

*Lord, may the candles we light this day bring alive in us the gifts of our baptism, to be caring like the Father, to be generous like the Son, to be faithful like the Holy Spirit.*

KEYWORD

*Welcome and celebration.*

**3**

If you think well of me I become better.
This was the secret of Jesus' teaching.
The Father of Love makes the sun shine
on the good and on the bad alike.

                              cf Mk 6,30-34

PRAYER     *Lord, we bless our throats today in memory
of your Saint Blaise and we think of those
awesome gifts of speech and song that can
bring joy to our world.*

KEYWORD    *Thinking well of us.*

**4**

Often we are not joyous persons, nor are
we lit up by the sunshine of God's love.
Plodders, though we may be, yet in
God's sight we are always a Light of the
World.                        cf Mt 5,13-16

PRAYER     *Lord, it is difficult to be a Light of Joy, if
one is not aware of your unconditional kind
of love, and if one has never experienced
love for one's own sake, how can one taste
happiness? So bless us as we wait in hope of
joy to be fulfilled.*

KEYWORD    *Love unconditional.*

## 5

Jesus touched people lovingly. He wanted to put people in touch with each other. He broke the ritual chain that would prevent him from touching undesirables.                        cf Mk 6,53-56

PRAYER

*Lord, it is often easy to keep in touch with those who like us and admire us. Give us an eye for the untouchables, the outsiders, the · strays, those who can never make it in life.*

KEYWORD

*Touching the untouchable.*

∽

## 6

When the holy monk with the cure died, people still came to see his cat for healing. Jesus warns us not to confuse God with unclean hands or religiosity.
                        cf Mk 7,1-3

PRAYER

*Lord, we can make sacred cows and cats out of religious rules and laws. You ask us to test our rules against the warmth of charity and caring for people.*

KEYWORD

*Sacred cows.*

∽

7

We always want to be satisfied. Jesus asks us to talk to the inside person in us, the Spirit that appreciates and says "I do not have to have more, I have enough. I have the sun, the sky, the air, work for my hands, food to eat and people to love. That is enough for me".

cf Mk 7,14-23

PRAYER

*Lord, bless all that I see, meet and think of this day. Open my heart to realise that the best gifts in life are free.*

KEYWORD

*What is enough.*

8

Jesus didn't want anyone to know where he was, but a pagan woman found him out, and he cured her sick daughter.

cf Mk 7,24-30

PRAYER

*Lord, I wanted to be anonymous on that flight. A sobbing woman sat beside me. Her newborn baby had died. She was single. She was bringing him home to have him buried with her people. It was a privilege to be found that night.*

KEYWORD

*Being found out.*

# 9

Jesus took the deaf and dumb man aside from the crowd. We can crowd our lives with overdoing things. Aside, in our own heart is God's Spirit. A rest there, can give new hearing and new speech.                                cf Mk 7,31-37

PRAYER        *Lord, with two ears and one mouth I should give double time to listening, but I can't really listen without your help. Take me aside to waste time with you.*

KEYWORD       *Take me aside.*

❧

# 10

Jesus gets the people to sit down. He serves their hunger with food. They receive all, unmerited.            cf Mk 8,1-10

PRAYER        *Lord, we receive because God is good. All is given, not earned. We are loved in our longing, hunger and weakness.*

KEYWORD       *Sit down, be served.*

❧

**11** Jesus sees our capacity for goodness first, and laws a second. He encourages us to be life-givers, to be reconciled, to be peace-makers. Then the laws fit into place.                                    cf Mt 5,17-37

PRAYER        *Lord, make me a life-giver with words, humour and human touch that lighten the burdens of people.*

KEYWORD       *To be.*

**12** God surrounds our lives with miracles and yet we ask for signs. The breath of life, the bread we eat, the crocus with its flaming heart, the weed with its golden cup welcoming the light. All is there for you and me.                              cf Mk 8,11-13

PRAYER        *Lord, open our eyes and our hearts to understand and to see the miracle of water turned into wine in the flowers.*

KEYWORD       *Wine in flowers.*

## 13

Jesus longs to give us an understanding of life, to see more, to hear more, to appreciate reality. Our greed and selfish thoughts get in the way. He does not want to see our growth stunted.

cf Mk 8,17-21

**PRAYER**     *Lord, give us a listening heart especially when you speak to us in the Gospel and when we meet you in the faces of people.*

**KEYWORD**     *To appreciate.*

## 14

A man cannot see people clearly. Jesus sends him home with new sight.

cf Mk 8,22-26

**PRAYER**     *Lord, the everyday people at home who encourage us, care about us, overlook our shortcomings tend to be forgotten. They are real Valentine people!*

**KEYWORD**     *Everyday people.*

## 15

In sickness, tragedy, death, new beauty can be born. Jesus will suffer grievously and rise again. Peter cannot grasp this.

cf Mk 8,31-33

PRAYER        *Lord, the cross of life does not release us*
              *from suffering. Because of you suffering*
              *isn't meaningless.*

KEYWORD       *Not meaningless.*

**16**        There isn't a pill for every pain in life.
              Jesus does not like pain or send pain
              but it is part of the road we have to
              travel. There are crosses of temperament
              and limitations – family failings, awk-
              ward neighbours, disappointments and
              the unexpected that we don't choose.
              What seems a loss can be growth and
              new life if we trust in God.

                                           cf Mk 8,34.9,1

PRAYER        *Lord, for what has been – Thanks. For what*
              *will be – Yes.*

KEYWORD       *Loss not the end.*

**17**        My hermit friend lives in the mountain.
              She calls the place "The Transfiguration
              of Christ". Her vision is that God is in
              love with the world, with all that exists,
              like green grass and flowers, puffy

clouds, chirping birds, mountain tops,
trickling water, ducks and hens, saints
and sinners. What I see as ordinary she
sees as extraordinary.          cf Mk 9,2-13

PRAYER        *Lord, the hermit says she is not lonely
              because of her awareness of your loving
              care, and in a sense she is in touch with all
              the world.*

KEYWORD       *Christ transfigured.*

&

**18**        Jesus suggests doing crazy things for
              love's sake, like not hitting back, lending
              generously, loving my enemy, praying
              for those who don't like me. I feel
              inadequate, but I am consoled that God
              is the One who is always doing crazy
              things for love's sake.          cf Mt 5,38-48

PRAYER        *Lord, a mother told me that she was crazy
              having the new baby when they couldn't
              afford even a holiday, but all worked out
              well. There is a lot of crazy loving in the
              world, like being faithful to one's partner,
              waiting on the sick, the weak and the
              elderly, being tolerant.*

KEYWORD       *Crazy love.*

&

**19**   Is our sickness dumbness of spirit too?
We don't talk, no dialogue. The result is
convulsion and pain, broken homes,
broken people, broken hearts.

cf Mk 9,14-29

PRAYER   *Lord, take us by the hand too. Help us to be
in touch with each other, with tolerance
and talk.*

KEYWORD   *Dumbness or talk.*

❧

**20**   Our God is a God of welcomes. The
Father welcomes the weak, the powerless, his little ones who have nothing to
offer except themselves.

PRAYER   *Lord, help me to know your welcoming
heart. To welcome myself as your gift, and
to welcome the gift of others, especially the
shabbily wrapped and the awkwardly
bound. Bless the children of our world.*

KEYWORD   *Come to me.*

❧

**21**   The Lenten prayer says, "Lord you are
merciful to all. You hate nothing that
you have created. You overlook our sins,
helping us to turn into loving persons."

God is all tenderness and compassion.
Now is a spring of joyful thoughts.

cf Mt 6,16-18

PRAYER        *Lord, Lent is about your love for me. The*
              *Father sees and cares. Fast, alms-giving and*
              *prayers are of value as ways of becoming*
              *loving persons, with ashes of tenderness and*
              *compassion that God desires for us.*

KEYWORD       *All tenderness and compassion.*

22   A woman goes through a kind of death
     to give birth, and the new life is miracle,
     wonder and beauty. Death and life are
     tied together in God's plan, and are
     present in human situations, our per-
     sonal life, our dealings with people.

cf Lk 9,22-25

PRAYER        *Lord, because of your victory over death,*
              *you give us hope, that even in the valley of*
              *darkness, in times of sickness and tragedy,*
              *you are present with us. For in you darkness*
              *is light.*

KEYWORD       *Death and life partners.*

**23** Jesus was a wedding day person with an eye for welcome, a hand for friendship and a spirit to celebrate.     cf Mt 9,14-15

PRAYER     *Lord, your way is to relieve pain. May we ease the burdens of people this day with a word, a call, a smile, a gift.*

KEYWORD     *Welcome.*

❧

**24** I remember Fr John's advice about beginning a new parish. "Eat and drink with the people first, before serious business." Jesus eats and drinks with us sinners first. There may be serious business afterwards to our advantage.
                                                    cf Lk 5,27-32

PRAYER     *Lord, you invite us to come, to take and eat, to share your table. We are never good enough – that's a trap. We are always weak enough – that's the truth.*

KEYWORD     *Weak enough to eat.*

❧

**25** That Jesus is tempted is a compliment to our struggling humanity. It is a reason for joy that God accepts our make-up as we are. God will not change us into angels of bread but he will help us to

grow in love through everyday decisions
we make in the imperfect situations of
life.                                   cf Mt 4,1-11

PRAYER          *Lord, make us grow in love, keeping an eye
for kindness, offering a hand to help,
encouraging those near us this day.*

KEYWORD         *Compliments, to the tempted.*

✐

**26** When we meet God we will be compli-
mented for feeding the hungry, caring
for the sick, visiting a prisoner. To have
neglected others, brings pain and hurt
on ourselves. It is not of God. God is
love and cannot condemn.

cf Mt 25,31-40

PRAYER          *Lord, help us to grow in love, to treat one
another kindly, to feel pity for people who
do wrong, to be sensitive, to say thanks and
sorry, to have the strength to be fair, to have
humour, to make joy.*

KEYWORD         *Growth in love.*

✐

**27** The Spirit prays through all humanity in
ways we can never fathom. Jesus tells us
that our prayer does not make God love
us because God already and always
loves us. Our prayers help to let the light

of God's love warm our minds and hearts with gratitude, hospitality, forgiveness and kindness.            cf Mt 6,7-15

PRAYER        *Lord, the Father knows what we need before we ask. But a helpless little child asking the parent for a favour makes itself more lovable and the parent more generous.*

KEYWORD       *The Spirit prays.*

28 Jonah refuses to talk of God's love to the Ninivites, because in his mind they were undesirables. He skips to sea, but God hooks him in the whale. He goes reluctantly, but tries to paint a bad picture of God. To his surprise the people change their ways and become a loving community. God's mercy is much broader than our small minds.            cf Lk 11,29-32

PRAYER        *Lord, help us never to lose sight of your mercy, to the best and saintly, to the worst and weakest. In the strength of your mercy help us to be compassionate in mind and heart to others this day.*

KEYWORD       *God of surprises.*

## 29

He took his own life last week. Was his understanding clouded? His will weak? Did he ever have the strength to ask, to seek, to knock at the Father's door who gives the Bread of Mercy to broken people?         cf Mt 7,1-12

**PRAYER**     *Lord, bless all in agony of mind who cannot cope. Bless their dear ones who are left with hurt, loss and painful worry.*

**KEYWORD**     *Pain of mind.*

# *March*

## 1

A child had a row with a neighbour's child. The parent went to court for a settlement. The child progressed happily through it all. The parent said, "I should have had my say with my neighbour and leave everything at that. Instead I made a mountain out of a molehill."

PRAYER

*Lord, help us not to make mountains out of molehills when we are annoyed with one another. If we knew all our stories we would be sitting down together, linking arms, drinking tea and coffee.*

KEYWORD

*Mountains out of molehills.*

## 2

Love does crazy things, like befriending enemies and making the sun shine on the good and bad alike. The everyday caring love of parents for young children is amazing grace.          cf Mt 5,43-48

PRAYER

*Lord, I received five letters of thanks from five confirmation pupils. Thanks is such a magic word. Why don't we use it more often?*

KEYWORD

*Thanks.*

**3** The artwork looked dull against the wall but when exposed to light it was extraordinarily beautiful. We hang on, plod on and feel dull and colourless often. But we are God's delight full of colour to be realised.                cf Mt 17,1-9

PRAYER *Lord, when we feel dull and colourless, we need a mountain experience of light. To be touched with affection, to be told we are lovable, to receive a thanks is a transfiguration.*

KEYWORD *Ordinary = extraordinary.*

**4** The frightened little rabbit, pursued by death hounds, jumps into the king's carriage for safety. The king draws his sword, but when his eyes meet the eyes of the rabbit his heart melts with compassion. He takes the rabbit home as a family pet.                cf Lk 6,36-38

PRAYER *Lord, we are hounded by guilt, suffering and limitations, but your heart melts with merciful compassion when you see us.*

KEYWORD *Compassionate eye.*

**5**

Our flesh and blood humanity, is the sign of God's love. Titles, clothes attracting attention, do not matter but giving attention does.            cf Mt 23,1-12

PRAYER    *Lord, you became flesh to ease the burdens of humanity, to give us your attention. Help us to be attentive to our own humanity and to the needs of others this day.*

KEYWORD    *Giving attention.*

❧

**6**

Be like the Father who saves us in all kinds of ways, giving us sunrise and sunset, the breath of life, food and friends. Serving can be thankless but it is rewarding indeed.            cf Mt 20,17-28

PRAYER    *Lord, let me be the first to notice others, with a greeting, with a compliment, with a word of encouragement.*

KEYWORD    *Noticing others.*

❧

**7**

One day during a famine, an African farmer sat on a steaming pot of food. He covered the pot with his cloak to hide the food from a visiting hungry neighbour. In doing so he burned his

backside and the food so that it became
useless for tongue to taste.

cf Lk 16,19-31

PRAYER    *Lord, when we don't ease the suffering of
the hungry with food, you certainly don't
burn us, but we lessen our taste for joy.*

KEYWORD    *Satisfying taste.*

8    The landlord rents out his property.
When the rent-man comes to collect,
the tenants beat him up. He sends more
rent-men. They are beaten and murdered too. As a last resort he sends his
own son. They kill him. Is this landlord
foolishly extravagant or crazy, to believe
in the goodwill of his tenants, giving
them every chance, or is he a greedy
landlord grabbing the last ounce? What
do you think?        cf Mt 21,33-43.45-46

PRAYER    *Lord, you are always extravagant in our
regard. You dote on us as your children
because we are your delight. Help us to let
the light of your goodness shine through us
this day.*

KEYWORD    *Extravagant or grabbing.*

**9** Rembrandt knew the foolish ways of youth and also the joys and pain of fatherhood. He paints God as Father, wrapping his arms around his lost son, who kneels with hair shorn off in a tattered condition. He paints pity for the good son that stayed at home, who kept all the rules, but is so resentful. The father loves both.                     cf Lk 15,11-32

PRAYER       *Lord, it was easier for the younger son after wild living to receive your love. The resentful stay at home, rule keeper found it more difficult to let your kind of love touch his heart.*

KEYWORD      *Crazy love.*

**10** Looking into a well of water is a mystery experience and awesome. Is it because our bodies are mostly water? Jesus says he is the water that satisfies all our longings.                     cf Jn 4,5-42

PRAYER       *Lord, the baptism font is made like a well of water, and the chapel font invites us to bless the world and praise the gracious goodness of God and bless one another.*

KEYWORD      *Well/water.*

**11** Naaman is an army man, hard hit by disease. He knows God as authority, but he learns to see God in the ordinary everyday flowing water of people and places; the unexpected and the unlikeable. He doesn't like being pushed around.                                    cf Lk 4,24-30

PRAYER    *Lord, you know our need before we ask, but you invite us to ask, to search, to touch water because it helps us and disposes us towards your goodwill, The parent enjoys being asked by the little child, especially when the request is for the well-being of the child.*

KEYWORD    *Searching.*

❧

**12** If we don't forgive we carry baggages of guilt and wounds of hurt. The good Lord wants to free our spirits; so Jesus says 'Forgive always'. Our imaginary enemies know not what they do.                                    cf Mt 18,21-22

PRAYER    *Lord, help us when we can't forgive ourselves, for hurt done to ourselves or to others. Often we do the best in the circumstances but have regrets and remorse later. When we speak our word to you it registers. You heal and renew life for us all.*

KEYWORD    *Sorry.*

❧

**13**   Jesus was breaking the law when he
spoke to strange women, when he
touched undesirables and said that
fasting without helping people is a loss.
Laws are meant to help people not
burden them.                    cf Mt 5,17-19

PRAYER    *Lord, St Teresa of Avila said we can't be
sure if we love God because we have not
seen God, but we can be sure about our
neighbour and the people we see and meet
in life.*

KEYWORD    *Love/Law.*

∼

**14**   Speech is an extraordinary gift, a constant miracle, a relief from dumbness.
Speech is meant to nurture relationship,
heal our spirit, encourage our heart. Not
for accusation, condemnation or irrita-
tion.                          cf Lk 11,14-23

PRAYER    *Lord, your voice, your speech, your word
speaks in your creation, in all that exists.
Help us to hear your voice, to speak well of
others and of life. Dumbness is failure to
praise.*

KEYWORD    *Speech.*

∼

**15** 'Love self', Jesus says. We confuse selfish love with real love of self. We judge ourselves harshly. We inflict on our-selves guilt feelings that is not of God. We tell ourselves that we are worthless, not nice, not good enough. We see God as threat rather than as friend.

cf Mk 12,28-34

PRAYER *Lord, to love myself genuinely I must know myself. I cannot know myself without your help. I am your choice, your original, your delight – warts and all.*

KEYWORD *Self love.*

**16** Someone praying got it all wrong. He put himself in the driving seat, neigh-bour and God in the luggage. The right prayer sees God's mercy in the first place and all else in second place. His tide of mercy carries us with all our frailties and limitations into the ocean of love.

cf Lk 18,9-14

PRAYER *Lord, thank you for giving us this prayer to your heart: "O God, be merciful to me, a sinner!" This is heaven's lifeline and home.*

KEYWORD *His mercy is everlasting.*

## 17

Patrick found God in the Celtic spirit and in the music of Ireland. He took what the local people had to offer and brought a new song and songster – Christ – into their hearts.

PRAYER     *Lord, you asked Patrick to sing us your song. God in every face, in every flower, in every tree. We see God with us in tragedy.*

KEYWORD    *St Patrick.*

## 18

The poster said "God could not be everywhere". So he made mothers and fathers who are God and home to us.
                                    cf Jn 4,43-54

PRAYER     *Lord, house is a place but home is where we are loved, where there is tolerance and respect for differences, where there is en-couragement and hospitality, and a feeling of someone for me. Your spirit makes homes.*

KEYWORD    *Home is someone for me.*

**19**  We complain about aches in the toe, until we meet someone with no legs. The complainers could not be happy for the man cured after 38 years of pain. They said he didn't keep the Sabbath Law. Evil and suffering we cannot fully comprehend but the sunshine of God's love caresses the world all the time in the people around us.          cf Jn 5,1-16

PRAYER    *Lord, tragic death of innocent children numbs us, but thousands of lights of kindness support, comfort and surprise us.*

KEYWORD   *Father cares.*

**20**  As a little child speaks intimately of his father, so Jesus tells "My Father goes on working". So do I. The Father raises the dead to life. So do I. The Father judges no one. Nor do I.          cf Jn 5,17-30

PRAYER    *The Lord is kind and full of compassion. The Lord supports all who fall and raises all who are weighed down. He is close to all who call upon him.*

KEYWORD   *Close to the broken-hearted.*

**21** Jesus is the window to God. Through him we see the Father, hear his voice, enjoy his presence and our poor humanity is caressed in his light.

cf Jn 5,31-47

PRAYER *Lord, when Moses pleaded on behalf of his obstinate people, you relented because you always back down before our weakness, failure and broken hearts. You meet our sin with pity not with blame.*

KEYWORD *Pity.*

❧

**22** "Where do you come from?" they asked Jesus. "Where do we come from?" the human heart often asks. If we know where we come from it is a great blessing for the journey and destination. Before world and womb we were in God's mind.

cf Jn 7,25-30

PRAYER *Lord, you have made us for yourself and our hearts are restless until they rest in you.*

KEYWORD *Come from.*

❧

**23** The authorities were the ones who wanted Jesus arrested. Not the police or the people. When authority puts itself

on a pedestal of doing wrong, it can
only topple or have eggs thrown at it.

cf Jn 7,40-52

PRAYER        *Lord, truth sets free and is not contained by*
              *arresting. You did no wrong but exposed*
              *wrongdoing that burdened people's lives.*
              *Help us to admit our own wrongdoing and*
              *need of forgiveness before assessing others.*

KEYWORD       *Truth and authority.*

24            The schoolchildren wrote letters of
              sympathy to the bereaved parents of the
              Dunblane massacre. When bad things
              happen to good people God is in the
              darkness, easing away tombstones of
              pain with kindness, concern, and friend-
              ship, loosening grave cloths of loss with
              words of encouragement and prayer.

cf Jn 11:21-27

PRAYER        *Lord, you open our graves now when we see*
              *your Blessing, when we let go of hate and*
              *bitter minds. You free our chains of depres-*
              *sion through expression that lets us think of*
              *the other obliging neighbour.*

KEYWORD       *Out of graves.*

## 25

The Sisters were happy this morning. There was an extra treat for breakfast. They were renewing their vows. Virginity is a kind of death, but our God is always bringing life out of death. Not only in nature, but in the lives of Sisters who give so much to make joy and happiness for others, and in the lives of people who cope with money problems, handi-caps, disappointments, setbacks.

cf Jn 11:41-44

PRAYER    *Holy Mary, Mother of God, pray for us sinners now and at the hour of your death. How good it is that Mary does the praying for us when we don't know how to pray ourselves.*

KEYWORD    *Death equals new life.*

## 26

The other side of death is Heaven. Jesus tells that he is our bridge over troubled waters. He draws us to himself.

cf Jn 8,21-30

PRAYER    *We hang onto life, are frail and vulnerable. When we unite our dependency with the Christ there is meaning. Lord, into your hand I commend my spirit.*

KEYWORD    *Draws us.*

**27** Gathered by his word we celebrated first forgiveness with the little ones. The parents blessed their little one with a thumb cross. The little ones blessed their parents with a thumb cross in return. We felt at home with God.

cf Jn 8,31-40

PRAYER      *Lord, thank you for loving me. I am sorry for not loving others and not loving you enough. Help me to love like Jesus.*

KEYWORD     *Homeliness.*

**28** We pass from death to life when we are concerned for each other. This is God's word. Resurrection and God are already with us. Whoever keeps his word will never see death.

cf Jn 8,51-59

PRAYER      *Lord, the seed that gives its life to bless the world with golden grains, never sees her own wonderful family, but she lives on in them.*

KEYWORD     *His word.*

**29**　John gets into the mind of Jesus in the days before Good Friday. He paints an awful picture of rejection. A story with waves of death, torrents of destruction, snares of the grave. I remember my priest friend's last words, "Have a drink with me. I am finished this time. I wish God would take me."　　　cf Jn 10,31-41

PRAYER　　*Lord, we don't like the fears of dying or death, but we accept, trusting in your word; that you will come and take us to yourself.*

KEYWORD　　*Fear not final.*

**30**　God gathers us together in Heaven but the gathering begins now with birth and baptism, in the ways we help one another, and are for each other, making a better world. This is never without struggle and tensions.　　　cf Jn 11,45-57

PRAYER　　*Lord, gathering people together for meals, for teams, for friendship or community is never without effort and disappointments. You have the master touch as Gatherer of people. Strengthen us with your Spirit.*

KEYWORD　　*Gathering.*

## 31

There is no Easter without a shopping list. Making life more livable for others is the way we bless people, and God blesses us this week through palm, passion, friendship, forgiveness and resurrection.                    cf Jn 12,1-11

**PRAYER**    *Lord, by your cross and resurrection you set us free. You are the Saviour of the world.*

**KEYWORD**   *Saviour.*

# *April*

**1**    Judas wants money for the poor. Mary wants money for perfume to scent her friend, Jesus. Our religious mind can sometimes hide envy and self-deceit. To be happy for another who is happy and to be sad with those who are sad is the genuine scent of God.          cf Jn 12,1-11

PRAYER    *Lord, if we cannot scent another with praise we don't praise you. Heal our envy with your spirit of joy.*

KEYWORD   *Scent.*

❧

**2**    Jesus was troubled in spirit, betrayed, yet John says this was his moment of glorification. Strange words beyond our understanding, but immensely consoling, because we are troubled spirits so often in the journey of life.
                          cf Jn 13,21-33.36-38

PRAYER    *Lord, thank you for identifying with our human condition and our troubled lives. You promised that all will be well, and that all manner of evil will be conquered.*

KEYWORD   *Troubled spirits.*

❧

**3** Why did Judas betray Jesus? Was he envious of his friendship with Mary Magdalene? Was he a thief? Or was Jesus too human and ordinary? Not religious enough? We betray ourselves often with envious selfish thoughts, and we throw stones at others when we judge them harshly.                              cf Mt 26,14-25

PRAYER    *Lord, there was betrayal and confusion at your Passover Meal. The first Eucharistic celebration wasn't all smiles, beauty or perfection. You accept us in our weakness. Help us to accept one another.*

KEYWORD   *Betrayed.*

&

**4** "This is My Body Given For You", are Holy Thursday words and words of our Eucharistic celebration. They are also the words of love and marriage, and the words of the everyday work of human hands in the making of a better world, in entertainment, in caring, from breakfast to bedtime, and in particular, when we wash the feet of the sick and forgotten, with kindness and remembrance.
                              cf 1 Cor 11,23-26

PRAYER

*Lord, the children prepared Easter cards for the sick, bereaved and elderly in the parish. Others entertained us with song, music and dance. "This is My Body given for you", they are saying.*

KEYWORD

*My body given.*

❧

5

He brutally murdered a priest, a young woman and her child. During his trial the priest's sister was asked if she was bitter? She replied, "If I cannot forgive I cannot live". Our God of surprises, forgives the worst. He wants to free us from the chains of unforgivingness and bitterness.                              cf Heb 4,14-16.5,7-9

PRAYER

*Lord, make us peace-makers in the way we think, in the actions we do, in our relationships with people, and in our care for this wonderful world.*

KEYWORD

*Peacemaking.*

❧

6

Death leaves a lot of unfinished business – raw nerves, family tensions, confusion and loss. Jesus releases his spirit to ease our pain of heart, to heal

our pain of mind, to comfort our
wounded spirit.                cf Mt 28,1-10

PRAYER  *Lord, give us strength to take up our duties
in life as our dear departed would wish,
and trust ourselves to your loving mercy.*

KEYWORD  *Not here, he has risen.*

7  At the first Easter, the first thought of
the women was a scented gift for their
friend. The second thought of the
women was sunrise and appreciation of
light. And their third thought was the
big stone, the obstacle, the handicap.
Our sin can never be a permanent
obstacle when we trust in God, the
Giver of light, of fire and love, the
Maker of new babies, spring fashions,
sights, scent and sounds.        cf Jn 20,1-9

PRAYER  *Lord, we sing "thank you God for giving us
life. Thank you God for giving us life.
Thank you God for giving us life right
where we are. Alleluia! Praise the Lord.
Alleluia! Praise the Lord. Alleluia! Praise
the Lord right where we are."*

KEYWORD  *Stones, not obstacles.*

## 8

God's first messengers to tell the good news of Easter are women, and our first thank you to the Lord was told by the woman who clasped his wounded feet.

cf Mt 28,8-15

PRAYER

*Lord, all pathways by your feet are worn. Your strong heart moves the ever beating sea. Your crown of thorns is every thorn that hurts. Your cross is every cross we bear.*

KEYWORD

*Easter joy.*

## 9

We cannot describe love, but we know when it happens to us. The Marys who stay with us when life is difficult, who cry with us, who do not want to possess us, who want our good, make it happen to us.                                    cf Jn 20,11-18

PRAYER

*Lord, you show us that real love expresses itself in human ways. Like the sun, it warms, radiates light, gives joy to our world.*

KEYWORD

*Seen the Lord.*

## 10

Jesus is present with two men, walking and talking but they don't recognise him. It reminds me of St Martin giving half his precious cloak to the poor leper.

That night he sees God wearing the cloak in Heaven. Jesus is present in the troubled and disheartened faces but something prevents us from meeting him there. The meal of friendship we call 'Mass' helps us to recognise and help the neighbour in God.

cf Lk 24,13-35

PRAYER    *Lord, through this sacred meal give us strength to please you, help us to care for one another and bring happiness to people.*

KEYWORD   *Meal of friendship.*

❧

**11** Jesus keeps his pierced hands and feet even after he is resurrected. Our feet walk the earth. Our hands make food, do work, make money, make joy. We run our fingers through each other with affection. God goes with us in hands and feet.    cf Lk 24,35-48

PRAYER    *Lord, you did not discard your human hands and feet. You transformed them. I have the world at my feet today. I have blessings in my hands to write, to phone, to work, to care.*

KEYWORD   *Hands and feet.*

# 12

We are always fishing in life, and sometimes feeling we have caught nothing. Fame fades, energy wanes. Excitement passes. But there is One who cares for us lovingly, not because of what we do or have but because we are fishers in the boat of humanity.                    cf Jn 21,1-14

PRAYER    *Lord, I know I am always your beloved one, despite the bad feelings I can have of myself, and the "nothing achieved" mentality. Your words, "Come and eat", are not an invitation to the perfect, but a comfort and consolation to the weak.*

KEYWORD   *Come and eat.*

# 13

Jesus shows himself under another form. Having an eye for other forms, and images of God, is a challenge of today. Greg Norman had the greatest golf round in history at the U.S. Masters. He said in an interview, "It was something within me."                    cf Mk 16,9-15

PRAYER    *Lord, the poet catches different forms of your mysterious presence. "I see His blood upon the rose, and in the stars the beauty of His eyes. I see His face in every flower, the singing birds His voice." All pathways by his feet are worn.*

KEYWORD   *Hidden God.*

## 14

Jesus keeps his hands, feet and sides after the resurrection but he transforms them. It is an immense compliment that God would wear our human clothes of hands, feet and sides.      cf Jn 20,19-31

PRAYER

*Lord, thank you for the privilege of touching your hands, when I give hugs, carry shopping bags, dress the children, make phone calls, write letters, play games, serve food and renew the face of the earth by caring for the environment.*

KEYWORD

*Give me your hand.*

## 15

The wind is as free as is God's love, and is as intimate and as ordinary as the breath we breathe. Jean is mildly handicapped. She spends her life in hospital. "Come and see my forever friends", she said to me. She showed me Josie and Patsy, two old donkeys, placid and pleasing, on a green patch of grass, and a cat sitting peacefully in admiration.
cf Jn 3,1-8

PRAYER

*Spirit of the living God fall afresh on me this day and bring awareness of your pervasive presence in all that exists.*

KEYWORD

*Wind of breath.*

## 16

Pain, fear, dying surround our lives. Jesus does not avoid the suffering of being lifted up. He tells us that it is not meaningless.                    cf Jn 3,7-15

PRAYER

*Christ has died, Christ is risen, Christ will come again. Lord, help us in times of darkness and despair. Be with us through days of depression.*

KEYWORD

*No shadows without pain.*

## 17

Jesus said, "God loves the world". God cannot condemn. We struggle to believe this extraordinary graciousness. It is so much unlike the way we think. Because we aportion blame and feel guilty, we often transfer our feelings to others. But this is not of God. It is the way we were shaped to think.                    cf Jn 3,16-21

PRAYER

*Lord, that I may see you as you really are, me as I really am. Your delight in your handywork.*

KEYWORD

*That I may see.*

## 18

Brendan Kenneally, the poet, speaks lovingly of voices – of childhood, of youth, of adulthood, of dreams, of the dead, the voice of a street, a river, a tree,

a leaf, a horse, a dog. Our voice is made
of a thousand voices. We dip into the
Word of God to hear voices, to behold
wonders.                          cf Jn 3,31-36

PRAYER      *Lord, if everything I noticed today spoke; if
every face I saw told a story; then I would
know you the Word made Flesh.*

KEYWORD     *Voices.*

**19**  It wasn't the miraculous bread. It was
his way with people. "Come in, you are
welcome, sit down, you will have a
warm cup of tea. Tell me about yourself.
Aren't you great! Leave the washing-up.
Thanks for calling." I like it when I see
people sitting at bingo. It is the only rest
of the day for many, with a cup of tea
served. God's meals are like that.
                                  cf Jn 6,1-5

PRAYER      *Lord, I was telling the little ones that you
are our special forever friend. You give us a
special meal, Holy Communion, because
each of us is special. You want us to warm
each other with friendliness. But they kept
asking me about hell, and sins, and death
and you being crucified.*

KEYWORD     *Come and sit down.*

**20** The boat takes me to the other side. I didn't make the boat or send for it. Sometimes our boat journey is short. Sometimes longer, always complete. The journey can be calm, rough or frightening. The boat always delivers to the other side, to the other shore, to the place they were making for.

cf Jn 6,16-21

PRAYER    *Lord, you made the boat, you made the sea, you made me. Keep me on course to that sunshine shore. Calm my fears.*

KEYWORD   *The other side.*

❧

**21** If we knew the story of bread we would know God. How many hands are joined in its making, receptive soil, sowing, reaping, harvesting, transporting, firing, baking, shaping, cutting, patting, carrying, storing? God's pervasive presence surrounds our lives in the ordinary.

cf Lk 24,13-35

PRAYER    *Lord, we break bread, to share with others, to care for others, to satisfy. You are our bread. A slice of bread is a daily miracle.*

KEYWORD   *Bread.*

❧

**22**
A slice of bread is a sign of God. There is beauty of sun and soil there. Beauty of patient toil there. Wind and rain have caressed it. Christ has blessed it.

cf Jn 6,22-29

PRAYER
*Lord, you are our bread. We break bread with grateful hearts.*

KEYWORD
*Thinking bread.*

❧

**23**
God is the baker, who sifts us, shapes us, fires us, makes us. We are not our own bread. We are designed for sharing.

cf Jn 6,30-35

PRAYER
*Lord, because you are our bread, we too are bread for one another. If we can help somebody as we go along the way of life, we are heavenly bread.*

KEYWORD
*Bread.*

❧

**24**
This is the goodwill of the Father, that I should lose none of all that he has given to me. All people will come home to God. God comes for us. We don't have to worry. We are never alone.

cf Jn 6,35-40

PRAYER    *Lord, we don't have to worry because of your promise, but we do. There is fear, but you took fear on board too. You keep whispering to us, "Don't be afraid". Lord, strengthen our trust in you.*

KEYWORD   *Don't be afraid.*

**25**    The A.A. programme helped Michael to break the chain of drink. He said, "I don't know God, but I recognise him or her in every happening now. There are no coincidences any more. There is presence." "He will teach you all", Jesus said.                     cf Jn 6,41-51

PRAYER    *Lord, awake us to your presence. Teach me your ways.*

KEYWORD   *He teaches all.*

**26**    Eucharist means thanksgiving for the Good Father, the God of bread. The God of joy, the God in the face of all we see, the God of sunshine, sea and rain. Sad that we look for reasons to disagree about small details at his table, rather than rejoicing with people for his generous banquet.              cf Jn 6,52-59

PRAYER    *Lord, may all who celebrate the Eucharist*

come to share the banquet that Christ has
prepared for us.

KEYWORD        *Generous table.*

27    The secret that God gave to Paul is that
Jesus is with people enfleshed in our
humanity. Eucharist celebrates God and
people. The Body of Christ. Amen.

cf Jn 6,60-69

PRAYER        *Lord, through the sacred meal give us
strength to please you, and to care for one
another, bringing happiness wherever there
are people.*

KEYWORD        *The Body of Christ. Amen.*

28    We admire the old gate that does its
duty faithfully. We also use it to climb
over, to sit on, and to touch. A new gate
welcomes life. The Master says, "I am
the gate, I have come to give life in
abundance."                  cf Jn 10,1-10

PRAYER        *Make us life-givers like gates, to be used,
but never used up.*

KEYWORD        *I am the gate.*

**29** Good Pope John said, "The true religion is the one that cares most for people". Gene drove us to church, but wasn't a churchgoer himself. At the traffic-lights stop, he gave money to a beggar requesting help. He gave more than I gave at church.                                    cf Jn 10,10-18

PRAYER     *Lord, you are the great respecter of persons. All kinds of sheep are your care. Even the black sheep is your delight.*

KEYWORD    *Other sheep I have.*

**30** Sometimes we get an image of God as superstar, doing the miraculous, the sensational. We even expect some people to be psuedo gods, coming up with perfection. Jesus says that God is in the silence of listening. What has a flower to say? What has the wind to say? What has a child to say? What has tragedy to say? What has my partner to say?                                    cf Jn 10,22-30

PRAYER     *Lord, I saw a drop of water under a micro-scope and dreamt of oceans. I saw a forest in a seed. Voices inexpressible.*

KEYWORD    *Listening.*

# *May*

**1** Jesus says, "I am a Light". Light is mysterious, powerful, gentle, full of the
wonder of colour and seasons, yet never
forces.                              cf Jn 12,44-50

PRAYER    *Lord, you encourage us to be light-givers, in
the way that we can lighten the burdens of
others. You do not expect us to be the sun.*

KEYWORD   *Light-givers.*

❧

**2** Two salesmen went to Africa to sell
shoes. One reported, "Nobody wears
shoes here." No opportunity. The other
reported, "Nobody wears shoes here."
Plenty of opportunities. Jesus experiences a lot of "no nos" in his life
through Judas, Peter and the authorities.
But he turned them into opportunities.
                                     cf Jn 13,16-20

PRAYER    *Lord, crisis means opportunity. Help us to
see our way through difficulties that happen
but are not of our choice or making.*

KEYWORD   *Opportunity knocks.*

❧

**3**   Some travelled long, some travelled short, but for each the mission was complete. We trusted the bus that carried us to our destination. Jesus promises to collect us, be with us and carry us to him.          cf Jn 14,1-6

PRAYER   *Lord, our hearts are troubled. We fear the unknown. Help us to trust you, who promise to accompany us through the tunnel of death.*

KEYWORD   *I am with you.*

❧

**4**   It fascinates John, the way Jesus could hide himself, in such ordinary humanity. "I've been with you all this time, Philip, and you are looking elsewhere for God who is Father."
                                  cf Jn 14,7-11.14

PRAYER   *Lord, you were so small, we could not see your large extent of courtesy. Manners may be formal, but courtesy is a heart of kindness, a graciousness that gives attention to the ordinary and simple things of life.*

KEYWORD   *Courtesy.*

❧

## 5

The little ones on First Communion day
encourage us to stand and stare and
celebrate. Like the new buds of May they
are bursting with life, delicate as lace,
exquisite, unfolding, so much hidden,
infinite, beyond us. God says "Isn't she
something to look at – isn't he something else" – bundles of promise.

cf Jn 14,1-6

PRAYER      *Lord, thank you for lifting up our hearts
with First Communion days. Joy is complete
when we can say 'thanks'.*

KEYWORD     *First communion joy.*

## 6

God's word is in earth and sea, in rain,
in crops that grow, in food we eat, in
happiness we taste. His word in Flesh
and Blood. Good news is remembering
God's words.                   cf Jn 14,21-26

PRAYER      *Lord, you never speak empty words. You
clothe your words with vitality, encouragement, compassion. Make our words to one
another, worthy of you this day.*

KEYWORD     *No empty words.*

## 7

I noticed tears at the First Communion
celebration. The little ones getting ready

for full flight, away from childhood and
home. What are the new adventures
ahead? Tears said, I am happy for you
but I will miss you.          cf Jn 14,27-31

PRAYER        *Lord, you understand our journey. Going
              away is growing from one experience to
              another, relentless. You have blessed us,
              because yours was a journey too, going to
              the Father.*

KEYWORD       *Growing is going.*

∽

**8**    The tree with its clustered family speaks
         of God. Poems are made by fools like
         me, but only God can make a tree;
         whose mouth is pressed to the breast of
         mother earth; whose hands outstretch
         in prayer; whose sap is mysterious air.
                                      cf Jn 15,1-8

PRAYER        *Lord, your gentle presence, like the sap of
              the tree, is pervasive and touches the small-
              est detail of our lives, a single hair, an
              eye-lash, a blade of grass, a silver speckle on
              a fish, the coloured pattern on a dog, a
              flower, a petal.*

KEYWORD       *A tree.*

∽

**9**

Dance, dance, wherever you may be, I am the lord of dance, said he, and I'll lead you all wherever you may be, and I'll lead you all in the dance, said he. I danced in the morning when the world was begun. I danced on the moon, on the stars and the sun. I came from Heaven to earth at Bethlehem. I had my birth.                                    cf Jn 15,9-11

PRAYER      *Lord, you like joy. You have made us for joy. When dark clouds gather, and our halos don't shine, remind us of your love and joy.*

KEYWORD     *Lord of the dance.*

**10**

One day Jesus said, "You are my friends". A friend is not blind to our faults, but is someone who bucks us up, gives a compliment, makes a laugh, sticks with us when the going is rough.
          Jn 15,12-17

PRAYER      *Lord, thank you for accepting me as your friend. Help me to remember, that having a friend means being a friend.*

KEYWORD     *You are my friends.*

## 11

A little girl asked, "Why did they kill Jesus?" He was a good person; but sometimes goodness annoys us. Jesus excuses us, saying that if people really knew what they were doing, they would not hurt. cf Jn 15,18-21

PRAYER *Lord, why do I not look for the good in people that I dislike, in viewpoints I don't share, in differences of nationality, politics, religion? If I only knew the full story of the other person I would be linking arms.*

KEYWORD *They know not.*

## 12

Wings without wind are not enough. God promises to be the wind, the breath beneath our wings. No breath, no life. cf Jn 14,15-21

PRAYER *Lord, you tell us of your intimacy and wonder in the smallest details of life because I live, you live, you in me, I in you.*

KEYWORD *Breath is spirit.*

**13**    The teacher liked to explain that igno-
rance meant ignoring other options and
possibilities. Why should I react annoyed, because the other person is off
form? Why should I refuse thanks
because the other forgot to say thanks?
Why be fundamentalist about religion,
politics, nationality, because the other
person is?                           cf Jn 15,26-16.4

PRAYER    *Lord, your words in our regard are big-
hearted, like a parent who says that the
mischievous child will be good, when he
knows and develops his sense. When we
know God the Father we too will act differently.*

KEYWORD   *Knowing the Father.*

ॐ

**14**    I watch goodbyes everyday. The parents
keep pace with the little ones walking to
school, but only for a while. Soon
they'll be racing away. We cannot be
clasped. Our journey is blessed. "It is
good that I go", he said.      cf Jn 16,5-11

PRAYER    *Lord, bless our coming and going. We are a
pilgrim people. We are your delight.*

KEYWORD   *Going is good.*

ॐ

**15** The focus on Confirmation Day used to be on the bishop, the priest, the teacher. It was a kind of awesome and fearsome ceremony. Now the focus is on the young people and their families. Young people today are uninhibited. They express themselves through art and projects. They are practically aware of the need for helping the local community and elderly people. The Spirit of God leads into deeper waters of truth, never static, always creative and full of vitality, anti-fundamentalist, open to change.                      cf Jn 16,12-15

PRAYER     *Lord, you remind us that your Spirit will always be leading us to fresh pastures. Why am I closed to new ideas, fresh initiatives? Without change there is no life. Spirit of the living God fall afresh on us.*

KEYWORD     *Truth is ongoing.*

**16** The feast of the Ascension consoles us, because it says "Nothing is lost". We cannot hold on to things, like youth or time. Our experiences are like water rushing to the ocean; so much of us is secret, silent, ordinary. A lot is never noticed, known, or appreciated. But all will be celebrated and found in God.
                      cf Mt 28,16-20

PRAYER

*Lord, fifty years on I found out why my mother called me Joseph. He was the Patron Saint of the religious sisters in my home town. The find was a kind of celebration of her, and reminded me of your promise to us that nothing would be lost. All is found in God.*

KEYWORD

*Nothing lost.*

❧

**17** Two miraculous putts won the golf game. But the joy was in my friends, watching, encouraging, and being happy for me. We need others for joy. God completes the joy that is always running from us in this life.          cf Jn 16,20-23

PRAYER

*Lord, as we wait in joyful hope, thank you for people who celebrate our joy, through births, marriage and success stories.*

KEYWORD

*Making joy.*

❧

**18** Going to work, going to play, going to marry, going to school, going to the doctor, going to lessons: we cannot avoid going. Jesus interprets going. I have come from the Father. I have come

into this world. Now I leave the world,
to go to the Father.          cf Jn 16,23-25

PRAYER        *Lord, I am caught up in this mystery of
going, coming from the Father with you
into the world, and going with you home, to
the Father in Heaven.*

KEYWORD       *What an exciting journey!*

❧

**19** Joy is a taste of eternal life. Joy happens
when we are appreciated, encouraged,
and someone is happy for us. Jesus
wants us to be happy. He calls us his
delightful sons and daughters.
                                cf Jn 17,1-11

PRAYER        *Lord, in your prayer to the Father you said,
"Let me give eternal life to all." Your* PRAYER
*cannot be refused. We are forever in your
love.*

KEYWORD       *Joy.*

❧

**20** The hermit said "She was alone, but not
lonely". Her solitude with God embraces
all humanity and the world. She is with
Jesus praising the Father.
                                cf Jn 16,29-33

PRAYER

*Lord, as long as there is life, we can never be alone. It is difficult for the bright new leaf to see its father and mother. It is so busy rejoicing with life.*

KEYWORD

*Be with.*

∽

**21** Edmund Rice was a progressive business man, married and father of a handicapped child. He became friend of the young who were weak and poor. He set up schools for them. God's love overflows when we respect others. Education highlights that our real value is in God.

cf Jn 17,1-11

PRAYER

*Lord, help us to know you, not as a remote existence to be proved, but rather in the centre of our being, which is also love.*

KEYWORD

*Knowing is love.*

∽

**22** We can find harmony in our life, if we relate to the Spirit of God in our centre, deep in our being. This is John Main's prayer teaching, using the word 'Maranatha' as a mantra to find stillness.

cf Jn 17,11-19

PRAYER   *Lord, without harmony in my life, I cannot find harmony in others, or in the world. You promised us this harmony, when you prayed – that we may be one as you are one.*

KEYWORD   *Harmony.*

❦

**23**   The prayer words of Jesus are alive with joy and hope today. "Father, I want those whom you have given to me, to be with me, where I am – to see the glory." Those 'given' are all humanity.

cf Jn 17,20-26

PRAYER   *Lord, knowing things about people, is not the same as knowing a person. Your spirit helps us to know you. The sign of knowing you, is always in the loving heart, and the caring action.*

KEYWORD   *I want them with me.*

❦

**24**   During my student days, when one was neither fish nor flesh, an outstanding happy memory for me was the visit on a football team to 'The Columbans'. There was always a great meal of welcome. There were no questions asked. One was just accepted for one's worth, with empty hands and empty stomach. Jesus

too ate first with his friends. Maybe
there would be business later. Feed my
lambs and sheep.            cf Jn 21,15-19

PRAYER          *Lord, we easily forget that religion is your
love for us, first and always. You celebrate
and compliment us. All is given. We cannot
merit or earn your love, only receive.*

KEYWORD          *After the meal, Jesus said.*

❧

**25** Terry's cancer left him speechless, and in
a semi-conscious state. When I spoke he
opened his eyes in welcome, fully alert.
When I offered a blessing, with assurance of God's love, he nodded
gratefully. When I said, "I'll be thinking
of you", he smiled in appreciation. He
died some hours later. God's Spirit
seemed inside breathing out and outside breathing in a fountain of living
water.                     cf Jn 7,37-39

PRAYER          *Lord, you use the incompetent and inadequate, to let others see your face. Your sun
shines on the virtuous and non-virtuous.*

KEYWORD          *Inside and outside.*

❧

**26** "My life is finished if I don't get this exam", she said. A beautiful girl with a bright personality and a gentle smile. I said, "It doesn't matter that much. Do what you can. You have lovely gifts, you can do well anywhere. Even without exam success." Failing exams can be an annoyance, but can be a blessing too. Jesus' spirit breathes on our wounds, healing stress, easing pain.

cf Jn 20,19-23

PRAYER     *Lord, your spirit breathes on wounded hands and bodies, and heals us with words of encouragement, gestures of kindness and wonder; inventions of science, humour and wit of children; sight, sounds and smells of nature; the variety of animal and fish life.*

KEYWORD    *Breathing/Blessing.*

∽

**27** In our street one boy owned a football. If he was losing in a game, he ran home with the football. Footballs are meant for joy and sharing. We don't have to be over-anxious about the ball, because there are other and better footballs in the Kingdom of Heaven, Jesus says.

cf Mk 10,17-27

PRAYER
*Lord, you know how we cling to things for security. I know all kinds of substitutes – reminders of you – but not you. Let me see you as prize, and joy, refuge, and strength. Things are good, but not good enough.*

KEYWORD
*No one is good but God alone.*

⁂

28 Eaten bread is soon forgotten. The generosity of parents, the sincerity of the teacher, the commitment of the leader. The parish church is always there, to welcome us when happy, to console us when sad, to be a topic of discussion when we feel enlightened, to be left aside and be taken up again when we are in the mood. "All will be repaid a hundred fold," the Master says.

cf Mk 10,28-31

PRAYER
*Lord, help us to be glad for the gifts we have, for the opportunities you have chosen for us in life. Everybody lacks something; so keep us from self-pity and self-importance that blind us to your blessings.*

KEYWORD
*Repaid.*

## 29

He lost the run of himself, when he got a bit of money, promotion and education. Making our authority felt, lacks reality, when we forget that God gives all, and being great Jesus says, is more about giving attention, than looking for attention.                                    cf Mk 10,23-31

PRAYER     *Lord, when the bit of authority goes to our head, enlighten our hearts, to see that we are poor humans, dressed in a little brief authority, that makes the angels weep.*

KEYWORD    *Authority felt.*

## 30

I watched a parent help his little son to kick a football in the park. He held the ball with outstretched hands, at an appropriate height. After many efforts the wee foot connected. They both rolled on the ground with joy. God likes us to share the joys of kicking.
                                           cf Mk 10,46-52

PRAYER     *Lord, you called the poor blind beggar to you. That struggling movement gave him a joy, a dignity, an importance. Let us not do for others, what it gives them greater joy to do for themselves.*

KEYWORD    *Calling to contribute.*

**31** A priest, a sister, a counsellor, spoke about their healing work with young victims of drug abuse. Their respect for broken people, had the strength of Christ, whose concern for his temple of abused people, makes him take on the uncaring traffickers.          cf Mk 11,11-16

PRAYER     *Lord, bless those who work with abused people. Lift us out of darkness that sees no hope. This day is your gift. Let us see its light and beauty.*

KEYWORD    *We are his temple.*

*June*

## 1

If I am trying to be superior, others are a threat. If I am wishing to know the truth, others are friends and helpers.

cf Mk 11,11-16

PRAYER

*Lord, when I am irritated by authority, is it an excuse for my own failings? Mistakes always happen. How to cope positively with the mistaken, has more truth than highlighting their wrongdoing.*

KEYWORD

*My authority.*

## 2

The twins wondered if there was any life after birth. When they awoke there was a new world. A father and mother, friends, sunlight, sights and sounds unheard of and unknown before. This second home was an unbelievable surprise. Our final home is the intimacy of Father, Son and Spirit – the ultimate surprise.

cf Jn 3,16-18

PRAYER

*Lord, we call you by three different names. You help us to talk to you in three different ways. We always bless in your name. To bless is to speak well of another. You have spoken well of us. We are here, in your world. Help us to speak well of you and one another this day.*

KEYWORD

*Father, Son and Spirit.*

**3**

We have tried. We lose heart. We feel rejected. But our mysterious God can take rejection, and still keep faith with human nature. Let us try new tenants. Life goes on despite the murders and the tragedies.                    cf Mk 12,13-17

PRAYER

*Lord, your mercy smiles on all that exists, and outwits our worst efforts to reject ourselves and others.*

KEYWORD

*Rejection.*

❧

**4**

The Wicklow Gap is the high peak of my visit to Saint Kevin's, Glendalough. I stood on granite boulders fifty million years old, and I photographed the past that I had left behind, miles of hills and countryside stretching through the plains of Ireland. I photographed the future that beckoned with joyful hope to the monastic city of Saint Kevin now hidden in the beautiful green valley that lay ahead. I thought of the millions of pilgrims, including Ciaran of Clonmacnoise, who came this way over thousands of years.

PRAYER

*Lord, Glendalough today was a heaven and earth experience. The monastery entrance arched with granite blocks; cobbled stones shone smooth with centuries of pilgrims'*

*feet. A lone man sat playing the maloden.*
*The rippling water caught the sunlight as it*
*sped over worn stones to its destiny. The*
*mountain was framed in colour by mystery*
*clouds and yellow firze. There was healing*
*in this air today.*

KEYWORD        *Kevin's Glendalough.*

❦

5    "How is God these times?" the teenage
girl quipped to the amusement of
friends. "How are you?" I asked. "Looking for a job for the summer", she said.
"I had a chat with himself this morning", she said. God our mystery lover
plays on millions of faces.

cf Mk 12,18-27

PRAYER        *Lord, help us to cope with the smart re-*
*mark, and to turn stings of conflict into*
*channels of humour and truth.*

KEYWORD        *How is God?*

❦

6    There were more people at Communion
because it was exam time. The presence
of Christ in Communion is a healing
power for his weary people, his Body.
Amen.                              cf Jn 6,51-58

PRAYER      *Lord, when we pray "Body of Christ, Amen", we express faith that God lives in people, his Body, and is also present mysteriously in Communion and Mass, also his Body. They compliment each other. Amen.*

KEYWORD     *Body of Christ. Amen.*

❧

7   We carry such a bad self-image, that the good Lord had to make a commandment to oblige us to love ourselves. Because we don't love ourselves healthily, we invent monsters and sometimes project our monsters onto other people, with word and action.    cf Mk 12,28-34

PRAYER      *Lord, you accept us because we are unique and special and original. Our failings and limitations are just ripples, lost in the ocean of your love. Help us to accept ourselves.*

KEYWORD     *Self love.*

❧

8   Jesus had a great heart and eye for the widow. Perhaps it was because he saw his own mother as a widow.
                                        cf Mk 12,38-44

PRAYER          *Lord, bless all widows in our world, who have given so much love and life.*

KEYWORD         *Giving with heart.*

❧

**9**  The ducks in the park are always entertaining. I could hear mother duck saying, 'Follow me' to the little one. Every movement, left, right, up down, round about, the little one excelled in performance. The Lord doesn't check on Mathew's worthiness, nor his exam results, nor his understanding of religion. He said, 'Follow me – friend'.

cf Mt 9,9-13

PRAYER          *Lord, your words, 'Follow me', have touched the hearts of millions, and led us to accept strangers, bear with difficulties and challenges in family life, in community living and in our working day.*

KEYWORD         *Follow me.*

❧

**10**  The wonder of my being is that I can be a grateful receiver, a gentle person, have a keen sense of fair play, suffer the pain of being a peacemaker, and entrust all to the mercy of God. Jesus calls this recipe 'happiness'.          cf Mt 5,1-12

PRAYER      *Lord, may your healing love turn us from ways of unhappiness, keep us in health of mind and body, and lead us to you.*

KEYWORD      *How to be happy.*

**11**      "We use only two per cent of our brain", the scientist says. We do need the love of others to kindle our light, to savour our salt, to refresh our spirit, to be welcoming and compassionate.     cf Mt 5,13-16

PRAYER      *Lord, you always compliment us. You only see the best in us. You look for excuses to forgive us.*

KEYWORD      *You are.*

**12**      Jesus understands our fear of change because of our insecurity. God is our only security. The way to live is to have an eye for one another.     cf Mt 5,17-19

PRAYER      *Lord, your name is love. Law and prophets mean respect for neighbour.*

KEYWORD      *I have come to accomplish.*

**13** Matthew was a money man and a lackey for a foreign power. Yet Jesus calls him 'friend' and eats with him. This Jesus who puts mercy before the rules is Matthew's new-found God.

cf Mt 5,20-26

PRAYER
*Lord, you put the law of love before the love of law. Prompt me with the instinct that wants to help another first, and analyse the reasons later.*

KEYWORD
*Leave your offering.*

❧

**14** "The red Sacred Heart lamp was like a brandy glass ", she said, full of welcome and hospitality. His Heart beckons with "Come to me. You are my friends. I am with you always. Be not afraid."

cf Mt 11,25-30

PRAYER
*Lord, help us to take the chill out of religion. Too much of rules, instruction, sacrifices and don'ts, make a stone of the heart.*

KEYWORD
*Heart.*

❧

**15** The liturgist was strict and precise during practice. "Where exactly do you place your hand? On the right or on the left?", he asked my friend. The Kerry-man answered, "in the middle, Father". Yes or no is a challenge Christ liked. We find it difficult.                    cf Mt 5,33-37

PRAYER    *Lord, thanks for the 'yes' you help us to say. Help us with the 'nos' that are for our good. Forgive us for our 'nos' that brought pain or unhappiness.*

KEYWORD    *Yes and no.*

∼

16    The eagle coaxes its young to fly, by dropping its little one off the wing, then catching the little one falling in confusion to earth. Our life too is frightening and exciting. But God promises to support us with providential wings.
                                          cf Mt 9,36-10.8

PRAYER    *Lord, because we are loved, you enable us to cure the sick with our love and care, to resurrect the dead when we raise the spirits of the lonely and oppressed, and to cast out devils that are of our own making.*

KEYWORD    *Raise the dead. Drive out devils.*

∼

*17*  I got a critical letter. The temptation was to answer fire with fire, or do nothing, and harbour resentment. The peace-maker, Jesus, says "Search for alternatives, like saying thank you for taking the time to write". I pray that nobody will be led astray from God by my limitations.          cf Mk 9,38-42

PRAYER      *Lord, I often think that the enemies you ask me to love are the nitty-gritty everyday irritations that come from people, plus my own limitations that shadow me. But you are present even in darkness. With you darkness is light.*

KEYWORD     *Loving enemies.*

❧

*18*  A street artist was asked to paint a canvas of the Last Supper feast for the king's banquet hall. The artist painted Christ surrounded by scruffy characters, outcasts, men and women, young and old, and a few animals to complete the picture. When the enraged king asked for an explanation, the artist said, "the good Lord makes the sun shine on the good and on the bad, and makes the rain fall on the honest and dishonest, and that is my understanding of the Last Supper".          cf Mk 9,41-50

PRAYER    *Lord, if we cannot praise something in the everyday person with all the limitations, we cannot praise God.*

KEYWORD   *His sun shines on the dishonest.*

~

**19**   There is a real me, an inner self, other than the show-piece of action or solemn behaviour that is seen. The Lord suggests silence for meeting the real me.
cf Mt 6,16-18

PRAYER    *Lord, to encounter myself, the counsellor suggested listening to the compliments I receive, and forgiving myself for not being perfect. May the Lord be with me.*

KEYWORD   *Self.*

~

**20**   God knows our needs and cares. God gifts us with prayer-power that disposes our hearts to his blessings.    cf Mt 6,7-15

PRAYER    *Lord, prayer that doesn't help to change my mind is dubious. May your spirit of PRAYER carry us in weakness. May Mary, our mother, pray for us now and at the hour of our death.*

KEYWORD   *Our Father.*

~

**21** I kept a gold sovereign in the safety of a press for years. It was an ordination gift from my father. Now I wear it as a broach. It reminds me of the blessing of family and friends. It points to the goodness of God. It encourages the interest of people.             cf Mt 6,19-23

PRAYER       *Lord, give us balance in our storing. Too much saving makes too much worry. Use before – and 'best before' is good advice from the supermarket.*

KEYWORD      *Best before.*

**22** I can eat and drink. I can dress in different styles. I can use my body to express myself in a thousand different ways. But who am I? This me, with all those different roles to play, all those voices to listen to. I am mystery, original and now.             cf Mt 6,24-34

PRAYER       *Lord, after the operation my friend said, "Being is more important than all those doings I have been involved in". "I am taking time from now on to smell the flowers", he remarked, "and be grateful for the moment that is now."*

KEYWORD      *Smell the flowers.*

## 23

A little boy is standing by the window of a blazing building ten stories high. It is dark. The fireman calls him to jump to the safety net below. The little boy cries, "I can't see you". The rescuer shouts, "Don't be afraid. I can see you."

cf Mt 10,26-33

**PRAYER**     *Lord, we are afraid. Help us to have trust that you will be with us always, even in the valley of darkness.*

**KEYWORD**     *Don't be afraid.*

## 24

"I have no problem with God", the lady said. "It is the people that he has working for him that irritate me." Jesus did choose funny people – money-makers, blunderers, traitors. The day I find the perfect church it will no longer be perfect, because I'm in it.     cf Mt 7,1-5

**PRAYER**     *Lord, the judgements I make on others tell me the kind of person I am. Scandals that put me off are often my own hang-ups. Because nothing can really take from my relationship with God and his goodness.*

**KEYWORD**     *Eye trouble.*

**25** Treat others as you would like them to treat you, is the pearl of religion. It touches everyday. It relates to all of life. It is open-ended. It includes all races and kinds. It is forever challenging to spiritual fitness. It is immensely reward-ing.                                      cf Mt 7,6-14

PRAYER     *Lord, I like to be treated with the word of compliment, a phone call, a greeting card, a gift, a meal or a drink. You treat me every-day with sunshine, the breath of life, the affection of friends. Help me to have an eye for treating others.*

KEYWORD    *Treating others.*

**26** People are like trees. All is received, and trees give so much life to our world. Most trees carry some kind of disease or are mishappen. Yet they fill the world with delight. They praise the day with their branches.               cf Mt 7,15-20

PRAYER     *Lord, we are redeemed sinners, and with all our misgivings, yet a delight in your family. We can make a better world everyday, being gratefully present to those around.*

KEYWORD    *A tree.*

## 27

The students celebrated leaving primary school yesterday. The spokesperson gave a long list of occupations that might hopefully come their way in life. There were three noticeable omissions – being a teacher, being a housewife or being a priest. Yet the real miracles are the real everyday caring acts of people. Glamour glistens, but can fade quickly.

cf Mt 7,21-29

PRAYER

*Lord, the true goal of life is doing the will of the Father. That will is full of concern for people, caring for the little ones, playing fair in business dealing, having a compassionate heart.*

KEYWORD

*The will of the Father.*

## 28

A baby needs the affection of touch more than food itself. Jesus is always expressing the love of God through bodily touch. In Christ, God touches the untouchable. A world without touch is a world without life.          cf Mt 8,1-4

PRAYER

*Lord, touch is a frail marvel of divinity. We have been touched with affection and love in many ways through life. Help us to return this gift through generosity and gratitude.*

KEYWORD

*Touch.*

**29** Eileen recalls her mother's advice when she was a young girl growing up. "Go out and talk to the strangers in the pub and serve them their drinks." We have to mix with people to understand, and the mix is never perfect, but rewarding.

cf Mt 8,5-17

PRAYER *Lord, help us to accept the mix of your people, before we know their religion, nationality or occupations. You simply care for the soldier, the servant, the mother-in-law in their need.*

KEYWORD *Needs.*

❧

**30** Small things make the difference. When she was baking brown scones, Vera remembered to include a few also for me. Mary brought a few new potatoes to a neighbour. John left some strawberries for the children, a surprise.

cf Mt 10,37-42

PRAYER *Lord, when people are good to us in the small ways of living life, we don't ask them their religion. We know that they have your Spirit.*

KEYWORD *The cup of water.*

❧

# *July*

**1** Doing the Leaving is an important exam. That 'leaving' never ends is a practical lesson. We can't hold on to childhood, teenhood, adulthood, time, breath or money. There is only now.

cf Mt 8,18-22

PRAYER *Lord, teach us how to leave things that crowd and clutter our lives and worry us. Help us to notice the flowers, to enjoy children, to savour today.*

KEYWORD *Leave for the other side.*

∼

**2** He was crucified between two thieves. He did not object to their company, nor give up on God or people or suppress his feelings of affection for others.

cf Mt 8,23-27

PRAYER *Lord, storms will always break without warning, and you will seem to be asleep. When you ask us not to be afraid, give us your Spirit of patience to be baggage carriers like you.*

KEYWORD *Storm and no warning.*

∼

**3** Two on a motor cycle shot a girl to death. Two in a motor car shot a policeman. We are not demons, but human beings who can do devilish things.

There is a cure for us, but not without a
price. The farmers lost their pigs and
Jesus is asked to leave the place.

cf Mt 8,28-34

**PRAYER**    *Lord, it is easy to blame others for the evils*
*of our world. Am I always leaving it to*
*others to care, and minding my own busi-*
*ness? Am I rather against the teacher, the*
*priest, the authority with "my Johnny does*
*no wrong, he is always right"?*

**KEYWORD**   *Creatures so fierce.*

*4* What we do for others, what we wish for
others, when we pray for others, counts
with God. The enthusiasm of the
stretcher-bearers, pushing and shoving
for a friend, moves the heart of Christ,
to make a paralytic get up, pick up, and
go home.                             cf Mt 9,1-8

**PRAYER**    *Lord, teach us to be grateful for getting up,*
*picking up, and knowing that we meet and*
*serve you in one another.*

**KEYWORD**   *Seeing their faith.*

**5** He had no problem sitting down to eat with misfits, strangers, moneymakers, ne'er-do-wells. Is his religion too Catholic for us?                    cf Mt 9,9-13

PRAYER        *Lord, we limit your mercy with our rules. But you will have none of it. It is mercy that counts, not regulations.*

KEYWORD       *He eats with sinners.*

❧

**6** "Having to leave things and die doesn't preoccupy me", she said. "There will be new mansions then, that I won't have to look after." "There will be new wine." So be happy for the day and make another happy.                    cf Mt 9,14-17

PRAYER        *Lord, they call you 'Lord of the Dance' because you are more a wedding person than a funeral person, with an eye for the joy of life, with trust in the Father who sees us as his delight and worth more than hundreds of sparrows.*

KEYWORD       *New wine.*

❧

**7**   The constant blessing of a parish is
children. When adults are preoccupied
with the worries of life and don't notice,
the children always see, and have welcome "hellos". The little ones in their
buggies stare at you with eyes full of
wonder.                    cf Mt 11,25-30

PRAYER   *Lord, you always notice and see us and give
us a welcome. You are always full of wonder
– a God of surprises.*

KEYWORD   *Revealing to children.*

**8**   A little child falls and gets a bump. The
mother soothes the hurt with touch. To
touch the dead body of a little girl or be
touched by a woman with a bleeding
disorder was against Jewish religious
laws. The love of Jesus for humanity
breaks through all such laws that burden people with pain.      cf Mt 9,18-26

PRAYER   *Lord, through the blessing of touch we
express affection and give love to life. Give
us awareness of this wonderful life-giving
power.*

KEYWORD   *Lay your hand.*

**9** Sickness, pain, death were always called 'Ould Divils'. Jesus doesn't discuss the prince of devils. Rather he listens to people with compassion. He touches their pain. He encourages our spirit to focus on the lord of the harvest.

cf Mt 9,32-38

PRAYER   *Lord, compassion was your cure for our weak and harassed humanity, not condemnation or rationalisation. Can I lighten someone's burden this day?*

KEYWORD   *He felt sorry.*

⁓

**10** Mary was shocked with Joan's miniskirt. John said, "If I had Mary's legs I'd wear a miniskirt too." We can be so preoccupied with our rights and authority over others that we do violence. The way we think can truly be our unclean spirit.          cf Mt 10,1-7

PRAYER   *Lord, when I see the attitudes we can have towards neighbours, politics, religion, I realise why your first blessing is to rid us of unclean spirits.*

KEYWORD   *Unclean spirits.*

⁓

**11** A garment made in China, Africa, or the Americas, contains something of another person's life – given for me. God's rule is seen in the life we give to one another, a helping hand to the sick, lifting the spirit of a lonely one, letting go the devils of depression and blame.

cf Mt 10,7-15

PRAYER    *Lord, you promise life – fullness of life to us. Let my life touch another this day, with humour, a word of praise, a call or a visit.*

KEYWORD   *God rule.*

❧

**12** General invitations don't grab me. The personal word does. With the personal touch Jesus trains his leaders. Real life is a one-to-one business. How to think of another, how to notice needs, having a desire to help, wanting to get close.

cf Mt 10,16-23

PRAYER    *Lord, you teach us to be thinking and practical, even cunning in relating to your people, but to be without bitterness, rancour, or envy, to be harmless with the simplicity of the dove.*

KEYWORD   *Sending you out.*

❧

**13**   Some people drop off church-going because it is trendy and cool. Fear is a big factor in life. They say there are no mean people. It is fear that makes us mean, so Jesus always teaches, "Don't be afraid". Be true to your spirit. Fashion and fancy fade and die.    cf Mt 10,24-42

PRAYER    *Lord, forgive us when we renege on truth, and let our spirit down. You always want our happiness, and you wait forever on our change of heart.*

KEYWORD    *Fear.*

&

**14**   There was an abundance of light last week, not measured or begged for, but given. There was a super-abundance of air to breathe, at no cost, and the rain spoke of water generously flowing – the price of life. God gives the basics with super-generosity. Why do we hurt each other, behave arrogantly, and act mean?
cf Mt 13,1-23

PRAYER    *Lord, you want our happiness. You wait for our change of heart, because despite our misgivings, and worst efforts, you promise a full harvest.*

KEYWORD    *Extravagant generosity.*

&

**15** Liveliness attracts. I didn't expect the nurse in the intensive care to be so pleasant. She encouraged me to visit the patient for a minute. The barman with the attentive eye, the telephonist with a warm word, makes a person feel special.

cf Mt 10,20-34

PRAYER  *Lord, liveliness is not something that we wear, own or buy. It is more than fashion or style. It is something inside. You long to give us liveliness.*

KEYWORD  *Losing life to find life.*

∽

**16** Two days before dying good Pope John said to his secretary: "When it's all over don't forget to visit your mother." Real miracles are being able to see the other person's viewpoint and to respond with sensitivity.

PRAYER  *Lord, we look for miracles in the wrong places. God is good and the neighbour is God's face. These are the basic miracles. Keep us from blindness of mind and heart.*

KEYWORD  *Miracles.*

∽

*17* Last week we twinned our parish with a poor parish in Haiti in the Caribbean. Today's news speaks a lot about marching in Northern Ireland, and little about 60 children who died in Haiti because of contaminated medicine.

cf Mt 11,25-27

PRAYER    *Lord, comfort all families, especially bereaved families. Help us to listen to those children's voices.*

KEYWORD    *Revealed to children.*

*18* Michelle scarcely spoke of herself, her pain or ordeal. She enthused about the new baby girl, and her husband. Love does make burdens light.  cf Mt 11,28-30

PRAYER    *Lord, there is no life without burdens, and no world of complete answers or miracles. But there is your promise of love to carry us through the difficulties and disappointments that come our way.*

KEYWORD    *Come to me.*

*19* Our young, and not so young, hunger for God – the God of the cornfield, that longs for openness of mind, and sincerity of heart, rather than the God of the temple with repetitious religious language, with overstress on rules and regulations, joyless and restrictive, rather than human and loving.      cf Mt 12,1-8

PRAYER      *Lord, life is lived not in the chapel or temple, but in the cornfields of everyday happenings and relationships. Give us the strength of responsibility in our friendships, in our love life.*

KEYWORD      *Cornfield and temple.*

❦

**20**      Glen meets many a crushed reed in her Montessori school for little children. There is no shouting or bawling, but rather deep concern for the weak one, and care for the difficult child that one is tempted to leave out.      cf Mt 12,18-21

PRAYER      *Lord, to follow you is to grow more human. You did not break the crushed reed, nor put out the smouldering wick in new found friendships.*

KEYWORD      *Crushed reeds.*

❦

**21**      The parish priest requested that there would be no sermon at his funeral. He said he didn't want one fellow lying in the pulpit, while the other was lying in the coffin. Only God knows all our weeds. Only God fully accepts us with our defects and our good qualities, in his mercy.                    cf Mt 12,24-43

PRAYER    *Lord, you did not object to dying between two thieves. Why do we get embarrassed about the weeds in ourselves and in others, and are so piously critical, forgetting that when I point the finger of accusation, three fingers are pointing back at me?*

KEYWORD    *Weed and flower in me.*

᠕

**22**    Jonah refuses to bring God's mercy to the despicable Ninevites. God enlightens him through the ordeal of suffering. The sign of God's mercy is crucified hands, open in welcome for saints and sinners alike.              cf Mt 12,38-42

PRAYER    *Lord, true religion is not in the sensationalism of secret messages, threats, miracles or visions, but in the wonder of the merciful heart, the compassionate way, that acts justly and loves tenderly.*

KEYWORD    *Jonah – a sign.*

᠕

**23** I watched the mother running anxiously with him, to guide his unsure peddling, on the new bicycle. Soon he raced away, out of reach. She had to let go. She became a caring bystander.

cf Mt 12,46-50

PRAYER    *Lord, help us to let go that too anxious grip on children, on people, on useless things or preoccupations. Encourage us to be interested bystanders.*

KEYWORD   *Mary outside waiting for him.*

❧

**24** God's extravagant generosity is beyond our grasp. Even though we are swallowed up with disappointments and feel sometimes that we never really made it, with debilitating sickness, and pressing problems. Yet the sea of his mercy prevails for us.          cf Mt 13,1-9

PRAYER    *Lord, you are fullness of mercy and compassion. You do not take note of our sins.*

KEYWORD   *Don't be afraid.*

❧

**25** The traffic crossed over the bird's broken body. There were thousands of white feathers strewn along, like snow petals around a grave. I lifted one feather to keep. It was so delicate to hold, a white marvel fading into a grey colour. Its base was wrapped in fluffy down, like a new baby's hair, that threaded into thousands of harp-like strings, and an infinity of harmony.        cf Mt 13,10-17

PRAYER    *Lord, I compliment the artist of this bird's feather. I trust that such a genius must surely be able to mend broken wings, and re-find lost feathers.*

KEYWORD    *The heart understands.*

❧

**26**  It is helpful to remember that Jesus' story of the sower sowing the seed, was interpreted by people in different ways, depending on their life situation. However its core message is that God gives the seed of life and mercy, and he also collects it – 'us' in the harvest, despite rocky and rough journeys.
        cf Mt 13,18-23

PRAYER    *Lord, we don't really produce anything, neither seed, nor earth nor growth. All fruitfulness is yours. The 100/60/30 per cent return will be our joy because it is your harvest.*

KEYWORD    *The seed is God.*

❧

**27** We don't give up interest in football because a player gets the red card, nor do we opt out of living because we encounter weeds of confusion, disappointment and disease on our journey to God.                    cf Mt 13,24-30

PRAYER   *Lord, you don't give us complete answers, in signs or miracles to take away our searching in this world. You do help us to face the events responsibly, with good heart and good will.*

KEYWORD   *Let them both grow.*

**28** She always carries the photograph of her baby in her purse. He died at childbirth. He gives her strength, he is always with her, she said. Her mother promised to go to church if God spared them. Her husband lost faith in a God that would let things like that happen.
                    cf Mt 13,44-52

PRAYER   *Lord, thank you for helping me to listen to the young mother with silence and awe. There are many roads to Heaven you tell us. Some find the Kingdom almost by accident and seem lucky. Others have to search and search, through the confusion of life and the grip of pain. You promised to be with us in every journey.*

KEYWORD   *Find treasure, search for pearl.*

# 29

Mustard seeds are insignificant; so are many people's lives. Leaven is an explosion of corruption – evil action that seems to invade life. But God's Kingdom works through both, and is not to be confused with grandeur and triumphalism.                    cf Mt 13,31-35

PRAYER

*Lord, we don't understand death. But you joined us in it. Your Kingdom finds us in pain and disappointment, in our own failures and inadequacies, in recycling the same old temptations.*

KEYWORD

*Mustard seeds and leaven.*

# 30

He played the trumpet at the wedding. He remembered only one story from the Gospel – the one about Dives burning in torment. He didn't want to know any more stories. He was right. The story was twisted from being good news to bad news, by inadequate teaching and misunderstanding.          cf Mt 13,36-43

PRAYER

*Lord, you are love, that cannot condemn, or send to Hell. Rid our minds of false images and idols of you. To follow Christ the Man is to become more human.*

KEYWORD

*Burning the weeds.*

# 31

Some marriages seem to be made in heaven, a sunshine relationship, plain sailing – treasure found. Others struggle, even break under strain. After trial and error the pearl of a new friend may be found.                      cf Mt 13,44-46

PRAYER     *Lord, the treasure of unearned blessings, the pearl that is difficult in life to find, are secrets of a God of surprises.*

KEYWORD    *Finding and searching.*

# August

*1*   Jesus never asked people to fear God.
He came to give life. God does not
condemn. He is Abba, Father; so the
burning and fire myths of a gospel story
are not of God's making; we punish and
inflict ourselves. God longs to liberate
us.                                      cf Mt 13,47-53

PRAYER   *Lord, why has the idea of a punishing God*
*such a wide acceptance? Is it because of the*
*desire we have to punish ourselves? We*
*carry huge guilt baggage. Save us from*
*ourselves.*

KEYWORD   *Fear not.*

*2*   Jesus' words and teaching have astonish-
ing impact. He makes the hearers feel
better about themselves. They sense
their value and dignity, because they are
sons and daughters of Abba, the Father
and God's delight.        cf Mt 13,54-58

PRAYER   *Lord, encourage us to teach our children to*
*pray and to pray with them. The child that*
*can pray, has an extra wing for the flight of*
*life and extra talent to cope with life.*

KEYWORD   *Astonished by his teaching.*

**3**

When Herod beheaded John to please a dancing girl it seemed like the end of a religious world, a death to honesty, justice and goodness. Yet it was the great beginning that introduced Jesus to the world stage. God uses the doom and gloom of the Herods for good and to confound the wise. cf Mt 14,10-12

**PRAYER** *Lord, the forecasters of doom and gloom forget that your goodness does not depend on us. Your good news is that the worst we can do only prompts you to give us the best.*

**KEYWORD** *They went to tell Jesus.*

**4**

Women and men don't easily forget food or meal time. The fascinating character of Jesus on the hillside was more satisfying than food or home. "You are weary and tired", he said. "Sit down. I'll serve you." Such extravagant goodness is a taste of God.

cf Mt 14,13-21

**PRAYER** *Lord, the Christian eye sees God as extravagantly good, who does not change or charge. Help us to give and serve from what we have now, rather than from what we would like to have. The giving heart grows bigger and knows God.*

**KEYWORD** *Sit down. Be served.*

**5** When they complained about Mary's miniskirt, John said that if he had Mary's legs he'd wear a mini too. It is the attitude of mind, the way we see, that makes the difference, not the externals of behaviour, food or piousness.                    cf Mt 15,1-2.10.14

PRAYER    *Lord, give us an open mind and a good heart. You help us to grow more human through all our limitations.*

KEYWORD   *The inside makes unclean.*

❧

**6** We feel alone at times facing heavy seas of disappointment and headwinds of worry. In the boat of life Jesus teaches that he is always with us, and is caring, even in the valley of darkness.
                                    cf Mt 14,22-36

PRAYER    *Lord, listen to Peter's prayer for us. Help us to trust that you will lift us up with your saving hands.*

KEYWORD   *Jesus held him.*

❧

**7** Her daughter's marriage failed. There was torment and pain. She met a new friend. Her mother explored every avenue for a church wedding. At the wedding dinner they blessed their new friendship with a prayer, a candle, and rings.                    cf Mt 15,21-28

PRAYER      *Lord, didn't you change your mind for a woman and a foreigner when she pleaded for her tormented daughter. Didn't you tell us that the Father has no favourites. There are no reserved blessings. The weaker we are the more your love abounds.*

KEYWORD     *My daughter is tormented.*

**8** The eight-year-olds have a talent for wonder and awe that delights. They pray naturally. They tell me that God paints the flowers. I have asked catechists to pray with the little ones in church for this First Communion Year. God did not make birds without giving wings for flight.                    cf Mt 16,13-23

PRAYER      *Lord, you give us wings to fly to you and cope with daily life. The gift of believing in a bird-maker and in wings that fly comes from you. It is the Father who speaks deep within the heart.*

KEYWORD     *Simon a happy man.*

**9** Being a virgin was a loss of life, a death, until Mary transformed that promise into motherhood, through the love of God. Virginity for love's sake is self-fulfilment and motherhood in a new way.                                       cf Mt 16,24-28

PRAYER *Lord, Mary was a self-fulfilled person because of her love for God and us. She became, and is, life-giver to millions of God's children.*

KEYWORD *Losing life to find life.*

**10** Are the young today irreligious, I am asked. Peer pressure and biological need make yesterday's moralising language for young people almost fruitless. It can give the wrong impression that the young people are not full of spirit. It is better to search for areas where the young are responsible and to praise their efforts.                        cf Mt 17,14-20

PRAYER *Lord, "mol an oige agus tiocfaidh si", means "praise the young and they come". Honey attracts better than vinegar. The eye that sees only the fault is a killer. The insight that longs to see and understand more is miracle.*

KEYWORD *Irreligious.*

## 11

The mother explained that her little child won't keep on his shoes. He kicks them off. They are expensive to lose. I wondered if there are things I could kick off too. Do I have to carry the weight of worry about tomorrow or the guilt about yesterday?                    cf Mt 14,22-33

PRAYER

*Lord, your little child laughed at me in his stocking feet. He knew that feet were more important than shoes, and when you trust your mammy with your life you don't have to be overwrought.*

KEYWORD

*God in the breeze.*

## 12

"I have all kinds of diseases and com-plaints", Mary said yesterday, "and I can't see or hear much. But I'm grateful for what I have. I'll just wait for the Good Lord. This is an envelope with a small gift for you. It is not much but I'd like you to have it for yourself."
                    cf Mt 17,22-27

PRAYER

*Lord, life deals difficult cards to some people. We can be handed over to circum-stances beyond our control – illness, tragedy, temptation, death. May your own handing over help us through ours.*

KEYWORD

*Handing over.*

## 13

The stray sheep broke its leg. The farmer carried the sheep around his shoulder for days. They became so close during the healing that the little one did not want to stray again dangerously.

cf Mt 18,1-3.10-14

PRAYER

*Lord, we sometimes wish to punish strays who hurt themselves and make trouble for us, in our family, in our world community. Do you really search for the stray in us with compassionate heart and fill your kingdom with the powerless and misfits?*

KEYWORD

*Searches for the stray.*

## 14

Peace-making is a blessed strategy – not peace-loving. The peacemaker takes risks, makes the first move, talks, listens, brings in a referee. The ultimate is when we can understand the pain of the opponent, see where they are coming from, shake hands genuinely.

cf Mt 18,15-20

PRAYER

*Lord, you encourage us to be peacemakers now, on this earth. There is no pie in the sky that isn't cooked on the earth. There is always a first step, a first move in peace-making. Let that move be mine.*

KEYWORD

*First move.*

**15** Mary cannot keep God's love to herself. When touched by love she hastens to visit her cousin, Elizabeth, who is expecting a child. Mary warms her with kindness, care and encouragement. She is truly a godsend.                 cf Lk 1.39-56

PRAYER   *Lord, Mary brought you to Elizabeth and the unborn John, even though they could not see you. May we too bring you to others through our kindness and helpfulness this day.*

KEYWORD   *She went quickly to Elizabeth.*

**16** Jesus speaks compassionately about divorce. It is not God's idea. But it is the human condition for many. "Not everyone", he says, "can accept what I say. Let anyone accept who can."    cf Mt 19,3-12

PRAYER   *Lord, there is no judgement in your words when you speak about divorce. You love what is best for your children. You have compassion when faced with our weakness.*

KEYWORD   *Let anyone accept this who can.*

*17* Children love to bless with their hands,
to show hands, to clap hands, to shake
hands, to hold hands. The joy they
generate during a Sunday celebration is
the explosion of innocence. The people
brought the children to Jesus that he
might touch them.          cf Mt 19,13-15

PRAYER     *Lord, we express love through the body you*
*give us. Help us to be affectionate and*
*caring.*

KEYWORD    *Body language.*

*18* The rose cannot keep its petals. We bless
the rose petals today in memory of Mary
– our special petal. Mary cannot keep
God's love for herself. She gives it away
with kindness and eager generosity to
Elizabeth and John, to you and me.
                              cf Lk 1,39-56

PRAYER     *Lord, bless these petals, children of the rose.*
*They beautify our world with colour and*
*scent. We thank you for the love you lavish*
*on us. Help us, like Mary, to colour and*
*scent this day with kind action and encour-*
*aging words.*

KEYWORD    *The rose petal.*

## 19

We long to be affirmed, rather than to be nagged, about what we should do. You are kind. You are good fun. You look nice. These are powerful helps. Be a life-giver. Be a peacemaker. The Master invites us.                    cf Mt 19,16-22.

PRAYER
*Lord, which is the better strategy, to play the ball or to block the player? To be for some-one or something has more joy than being against.*

KEYWORD
*Enter life.*

## 20

Money is good, but not good enough to satisfy the human spirit. Money cannot buy life, friendship, green leaves, butter-flies or sunshine. Money is a good servant, but a greedy master.
                          cf Mt 19,23-30

PRAYER
*Lord, help us to use wisely the blessings of this life, for our good and the glory of God's Kingdom. We are only what we can carry with us.*

KEYWORD
*What are we to have?*

**21** His girlfriend had a baby prematurely. He abandoned the girl and his baby. Eight months later he came back to apologise, offering to take responsibility, and hoping that their relationship would heal. Some arrive late in God's Kingdom. The only certainty is God's extravagant goodness and mercy.

cf Mt 20,1-16

PRAYER    *Lord, the good thief stole Heaven in his last moments. The truth is that Heaven is given to us totally free, all the time. We don't have to steal, only accept the invitation.*

KEYWORD   *I am good.*

**22** God does not wait to crown us for our good deeds. God waits to forgive us our sins and press us close to the heart like little children who long to be loved. All is invitation.          cf Mt 22,1-14

PRAYER    *Lord, did Matthew, your scriptwriter have a hang-up about judgement and grinding of teeth? Did he too have difficulty accepting that the poor and misfits qualify for Heaven? Did he too have to learn that it is our need that attracts divine mercy, not our virtue?*

KEYWORD   *Invites all.*

**23**    To be heavenly-minded, but of no
earthly use, is not the way of Jesus.
Sometimes heavenly-minded people
regarded the lame, the blind, the misfit
as unworthy of God's Kingdom. So Jesus
stresses that love of neighbour itself is
proof of God's love.          cf Mt 22,34-40

PRAYER    *Lord, love is not an easy word to understand. It is about decision, more than
feeling. Doing the ordinary loving everyday
actions for family, spouse, friend or stranger.*

KEYWORD   *Love the neighbour.*

**24**    You and I are special, not because of
anything we do, or the position we
hold. Nobody has your eyes, hands,
hair, voice or laugh. Nobody will talk,
walk, think, work like you. You are an
original, unique, a single mould.
                              cf Mt 23,1-12

PRAYER    *Lord, it is your goodness that makes me
special. You alone are the Father and
Master. You don't ask me to save the world.
Help me to do the job you want this day.*

KEYWORD   *One Master and Father.*

**25** I marvel at the spark of love that keeps marriages going through all kinds of difficulties, that makes friendship faithful, when there are other easy options, and make the heart do crazy things.                    cf Mt 16,13-30

PRAYER    *Lord, the spark of Christian faith is believing in Jesus Christ. It is a spark in the heart rather than logic in the head and it makes us want to help another, bear with differences in people.*

KEYWORD   *You are the Son of the living God.*

❧

**26** The old priest was tired listening to a long monotonous list of boring sins. He said, "Ah, stop boasting. Go and love someone, for God's sake!"
                                   cf Mt 23,13-22

PRAYER    *Lord, help us to stop boasting about our sin or virtue. It is a self-indulgence. Let us look to the One who knows us better than we know ourselves, the One who believes in the forgiveness of sin, not sin. Sin is lost and forgotten in a sea of mercy.*

KEYWORD   *Blind guides.*

❧

**27** If the camera lens is not working, our picture of the world will be murky. We can change our minds, clean our heart-lens and our perception, despite the stains we carry with us. We are spirit, persons with inner power.

cf Mt 23,23-26

PRAYER    *Lord, the happenings of life we often see as obstacles rather than opportunities. Is it because we cannot change our perception? You encourage us to think differently, change direction and find a new insight about self, our world, this day, the neighbour, and God.*

KEYWORD   *Clean the inside.*

**28** "I have no problem with God", she said. "It is the crowd he has working for him that annoys me." Strange that the good Lord can bear with our sin and hypocrisy and wait for change. It is we that call names.          cf Mt 23,27-32

PRAYER    *Lord, you tolerate the sinner and forget the sin. We can't see that the hypocrite is also your chosen one – a unique, special person. Such vision is born of the spirit in us.*

KEYWORD   *Inside you are.*

**29** He was lecturing on good business management. He asked his audience to imagine the speeches they would like to hear about themselves on their funeral day. He said that "in those speeches you will find your meaning of success".

cf Mt 24,42-51

PRAYER    *Lord, we all want to climb the ladder of success. But if the wall supporting the ladder is not made from your goodness and concern for people, then we're climbing in the wrong direction.*

KEYWORD    *The hour.*

❧

**30** Brian Keenan, the hostage survivor, looked at his hands and said, "There is a foolish hand and there is a wise hand." The wise hand is ready to give, to forgive, to be thoughtful. The foolish hand is careless, hurtful and selfish. Which hand controls my life?      cf Mt 25,1-13

PRAYER    *Lord, in the football game of life it is foolish to be thinking too much about the final whistle. It is wiser to be ready for the next pass that comes, from the give and take with others this day.*

KEYWORD    *Foolish or sensible.*

❧

# 31

The master that throws out his servant
for squandering his talent is not the
God that Jesus teaches. The God of Jesus
goes after the lost one, searches and
waits and rejoices when his mischievous
ones are happy.          cf Mt 25,14-30

PRAYER          *Lord, you must prefer squandering to
hoarding. You continue to squander love
and life on us without charge. Your sun is
our gold – everyday.*

KEYWORD          *He entrusts to us.*

*September*

*1*  The wise hand can paint, play music, write, cuddle a baby, prepare food, shake hands. The foolish hand is a closed fist that hurts, vandalises, destroys. The struggle to be the wise hand is the way of Jesus Christ.

cf Mt 16,21-27

PRAYER  *Lord, giving away and giving way is not loss but growth in human life. When we see parents and people giving endless time, thought, patience, and encouragement to those they live with and care for, we see not loss but gain.*

KEYWORD  *Losing life to find life.*

⁓

*2*  I waited in the X-ray room with a certain anxiety. I wondered about the healing and good news the Lord promised. Images of the morning flashed to mind, the concern of the night nurse, the bright smile of the day nurse, the calm professionalism of the consultant, the wit of the lady tidying the room, the variety of the food menu, the kindness and reassuring attitude of the X-ray team, the trolley man who wheeled me back, my friend and sister who waited, the professor who guided my craft.

cf Lk 4,16-30

PRAYER      *Lord, your spirit comforts the world through the minds, hearts, and hands of human beings. You are with us always through the people in our lives.*

KEYWORD     *I was sent to bring good news.*

❧

**3**   The leaves peeping through the hospital window seemed calm, but looked lonely. Yet they were not alone. They were supported by caring branches, rooted to mother earth, caressed in light, breathing air. "I am with you always", he said. You can never be alone.                    cf Lk 4,31-37.

PRAYER      *Lord, a demon of life is to think we are alone or lost. To give joy where there is none is magic that restores my own.*

KEYWORD     *What do you want with us?*

❧

**4**   In conversation we are often more preoccupied with our reply than listening to the other person. Real listening is wanting to understand the other person. Was this the wonderful attraction of Jesus Christ? His listening with such

understanding made people feel good
and do good.                    cf Lk 4,38-44

PRAYER        *Lord, you laid your hand on every single
              sick person. How we grow in stature when
              we get the personal word, the personal
              touch, attention and compliment. Life is at
              its best.*

KEYWORD       *Mary.*

&

**5**   I wanted a young adult to read on
        Sundays at Mass. Various appeals did
        not seem to work. One night in the
        local pub a young lady came to me with
        a humble request, "I would love to read
        at Mass on Sundays." God catches us in
        all kinds of different and surprising
        ways. Why should we lose heart?
                                    cf Lk 5,1-11

PRAYER        *Lord, I had forgotten that you gave us
              Annie who died today, leaving us shattered
              and heartbroken. She was a good, caring
              and generous person. I'm glad for her joy
              now. Help us to trust your loving providence
              that always provides for your children.*

KEYWORD       *Completely overcome by the unexpected.*

&

**6** The friends of Jesus are criticised for eating and drinking, instead of praying and fasting – on a Sunday. Jesus says, "You forget that religion and God is a wedding affair". God loves us. This is joy to celebrate. Maybe we need new specs' to see this kind of way.     cf Lk 5,33-39

PRAYER     *Lord, maybe our seeing glasses have got out of focus. Open our mind and heart to a better vision of God and each other.*

KEYWORD     *Yours go on eating and drinking.*

**7** Feed the hungry is a first prayer. Parents are very faithful to this prayer everyday. When a faraway neighbour is starving or undernourished we cannot eat full meals peacefully. Real prayer prompts us to feed the others.     cf Lk 6,1-5

PRAYER     *Lord, a pompous man asked a crippled boy why he believed in a God that left him hungry and poor. The boy said, "Sir, God did give the blessings of food and gifts for us to others, but they forgot to share."*

KEYWORD     *What David did when hungry.*

**8** There are four kinds of listeners, the book said. First, those who don't listen at all; they just wait to give their reply. Second, those who pretend to listen. Third, those who pick up a word here and there; like a child telling a story. Fourth, those who listen, wanting to understand the other person. The last is real humanity and sainthood.

PRAYER  *Lord, because Mary listened, this world was flooded with blessings. May her prayers help us to listen to my family, my friend, my child, my neighbour, the stranger I meet this day.*

KEYWORD  *Listening.*

**9** The man's right hand was withered. It seems that his heart had withered too. He had given up on life, left with no standing or stature. Jesus empowers him to stand as a human being, to respect himself, to face the fortunes and misfortunes of life.                      cf Lk 6,6-11

PRAYER  *Lord, the poet said, "you don't take people out of slums, you take slums out of people", then they take themselves out of the slums of fear, depression, jealousy and worthlessness.*

KEYWORD  *Stand up!*

## 10

To familiarise the First Communion children with Sunday Mass, and the celebration of the Sacrament of Forgiveness, I accepted the help of Cathy. She brings the children from the school to the parish church regularly through the year. She shows them the way we celebrate at Mass, using our hands, and the welcome greeting in the Sacrament of Forgiveness.                    cf Lk 6,17-19

PRAYER          *Lord, we bless at Mass to praise the wonder of you, in three different ways – Father, Son and Spirit. We bless our forehead, lips and heart to help us greet your word. We lift our hands in thanks. We shake hands to promise peace. We cup our hands to welcome Jesus – our friend, the Bread of Life.*

KEYWORD         *He came with them.*

~

## 11

A friend suffers greatly because she defends the poor and the unjustly-treated. I wonder how she can be so happy. When the heart is right with God, then criticism by other people doesn't matter that much.

cf Lk 6,20-26

PRAYER          *Lord, you loved people, but did not seem to need people as the reason for happiness.*

*Integrity with God is the source of happiness always. We can never be alone then.*

KEYWORD     *Those who weep shall laugh.*

**12**    Water, lake, rock in St Kevin's Glendalough soothes the spirit. The pilgrim is asked to throw an old stone, or a piece of dead wood into the water. It ripples for a second and is lost in an ocean of mystery. Can we throw off stones that drag us down with bitterness and hate, and rid ourselves of rotten wood that kills our spirit?

PRAYER     *Lord, are these words really yours, that you are kind "to the ungrateful and the wicked"? You are the compassionate Father. You are the ocean of mercy. You forget our sin.*

KEYWORD     *Love your enemy.*

**13**    My friend forgot to bring her spectacles with her. She borrowed mine to read the menu. "They're no good", she said. They were wrong for her. I cannot impose my spectacles on the world. Why am I so sure my views are the right ones for everyone else?      cf Lk 6,39-42

PRAYER     *Lord, you respect differences because you*

*made every single person different; indeed
every blade of grass. Help us to respect the
other's viewpoint, and to see difference as
colour in life, rather than an obstacle or a
threatening cloud.*

KEYWORD     *Take the plank out of your eye.*

**14** A man in love, living in a hovel, is often
happier than a loveless millionaire,
living in a mansion. The heart is might-
ier than possessions. The heart is a
lonely hunter. Only God can satisfy it
totally.                         cf Lk 6,43-49

PRAYER     *Lord, help us to put heart into our thoughts
this day; so that those we meet, greet and
think of, may be the better for our meeting.*

KEYWORD     *What fills his heart.*

**15** The baby was christened yesterday. The
father never showed up. The relationship was off she said. She admired his
mother for coming to the celebration.
She talked about the wonder and beauty
of the baby. She said that his lack of
support would make her double her
efforts to love this child. She had got a
job now. She had a small place of her

own. She had her friends. Such forgiveness and love of heart is godlike.

cf Mt 18,21-35

PRAYER        *Lord, to err is human, to forgive is divine.*
*Help us to be fair in our responses to the*
*challenges of life.*

KEYWORD       *Give me time I will pay.*

❧

**16** He was not of the Jewish religion. He
did not follow the Christ. But he was
praised for his honesty and concern. He
had a godlike heart. He gave us our best
prayer, "Lord, I am not worthy that you
enter my house, only say the word, I
shall be healed".                    cf Lk 7,1-10

PRAYER        *Lord, when we meet for the Meal we wait*
*for one another, St Paul says. Bless our*
*waiting this day, at work, in traffic, at the*
*shops, in joy and sadness.*

KEYWORD       *I am not worthy.*

❧

**17** St Teresa of Avila said that if her spiritual director was less holy, she could talk
to him. A broken-hearted widow, a dead
young man, onlookers, felt that they
could talk to Jesus Christ.    cf Lk 7,11-17

PRAYER      *Lord, the adults often look so worried and*
            *carry a silent stare. The children look*
            *directly, love to be greeted and to talk.*
            *Renew our childlike spirits this day.*

KEYWORD     *Everyone was filled with awe.*

&

18    It is the person who understands our
      condition, feels what we are going
      through, that attracts. He was called, "a
      glutton, a drunkard, a friend of prosti-
      tutes". Christ tasted the depths of our
      humanity and keeps faith in us.

                                          cf Lk 7,31-35

PRAYER      *Lord, Matt had a heart of gold and was*
            *kindness itself. His language was a little*
            *shocking. An apparent failing was, in fact,*
            *a great blessing that put people at ease,*
            *made humour, lightened the burdens of*
            *living for people.*

KEYWORD     *A glutton, a drunkard.*

&

19    "The woman with a bad name has great
      heart", Jesus says. How could she give
      such affectionate attention to another,
      without being greatly loved herself?

                                          cf Lk 7,36-50

PRAYER    *Lord, the love of woman is a mirror of your
          own divine love. While we wait for the
          marriage feast of heaven, you give us the
          love of woman to bless our world.*

KEYWORD   *Do you see this woman?*

❧

**20**  The church that Jesus gathered around
        him to teach, preach and heal wasn't a
        male-only church. St Luke mentions the
        names of the women with Jesus: Mary,
        Joanne, Suzanne. They weren't too pious
        or immaculate. They had lovely human-
        ity that attracted people to God.

        cf Lk 8,1-3

PRAYER    *Lord, today we see emerging again a picture
          of a church that respects equality. We are all
          brothers and sisters. You are Father of us all.
          You bring us together to this table and ask
          us to do what you did.*

KEYWORD   *Certain women with him.*

❧

**21**  A seed depends on mother earth, sun-
        shine and rain, to reveal its secrets. God
        chose to depend on us – our hands to
        make a better world, when we feed his
        people and care for one another.

        cf Lk 8,4-15

**PRAYER**  *Lord, your word becomes flesh everyday,*
*when we see and speak to one another,*
*become friends, share our joys and sorrows.*

**KEYWORD**  *Seed is the word of God.*

❧

**22**  The way to treat children fair is to treat
them differently. Each of us is different.
God treats us differently for love's sake
too. We sometimes cry 'foul' when the
thief gets to Heaven. How can misfits
and ne'er-do-wells be God's friends?
God's story is beyond reason, because it
is about crazy love for his people.

cf Mt 20,1-16

**PRAYER**  *Lord, a junior infant sent me an art card of*
*thanks after our Mass of St Ciaran. He*
*drew a man with two huge arms and hands*
*outstretched in welcome and joy, supported*
*by a small altar. The wonder of this message*
*was beyond reason. It caught the meaning*
*of being Christian.*

**KEYWORD**  *Why be envious because I'm generous?*

❧

**23**  We are not asked to make light. God
does that. We are asked to share it, to be
lampstands, that give a little help,

support, direction, enlightenment to
others on a journey of life.

cf Lk 8,16-18

PRAYER        *Lord, a little child does not complain about
the quality of the lampstand, provided he
can read his book. We are lampstands of
joy, generosity and wonder. Let us share
with others this day.*

KEYWORD        *Lampstands.*

❧

24        They never realised that the little boy
was short-sighted, until they brought
him to the doctor. His face lit with joy,
when a bright world of faces in focus,
happened with the new glasses. Our
seeing needs to be supported with the
effort of searching, listening and doing.

cf Lk 8,19-21

PRAYER        *Lord, faith is the way we see life. You give
this gift of sight. But it needs tolerance,
compassion, and a sense of gratitude to
bring it into good focus.*

KEYWORD        *They want to see you.*

❧

**25** God gives all, and promises to heal all humanity. This is the good news. We are givers of life when we give attention to people and try to understand their needs and problems.                     cf Lk 9,1-6

PRAYER  *Lord, the good news is your love for us. If the sun shines renewing the world every second, why should I forget sun-days because others forget?*

KEYWORD  *Proclaim good news.*

❧

**26** Life is puzzling for us too. We want to see more. St Patrick put Christ in the centre of the puzzle of life. This is the Celtic cross.                     cf Lk 9,7-9

PRAYER  *Lord, help us to see that life is never meaningless, because of what you have done. Failure and death you transform. The drudgery of life you bless.*

KEYWORD  *Herod puzzled and anxious to see Jesus.*

❧

**27** When we see a Church suffering through human frailty, rejected for outmoded ideas, with vacant places in seminaries, convents and chapels, are we like Peter or the press saying, "Lord,

this could not happen to you." We
forget that it's the price of being re-
newed.                              cf Lk 9,18-22

PRAYER        *Lord, a little child learning to walk stum-
              bles, falls and makes trouble. It's the price of
              life. By your Cross and Resurrection you set
              us free. You are the Saviour of the world.*

KEYWORD       *To suffer grievously and to be raised again.*

❧

**28**  There is a helplessness in the human
condition, waiting for months, sometimes for years to die, waiting in prison,
waiting for change in a disturbed mind,
waiting with nightmares of fear. It is as
if we are handed over to the unknown.
It is passion time.              cf Lk 9,43-45

PRAYER        *Lord, you tell us you were handed over. You
              accept the depths of our helplessness, the
              passion of our waiting, trusting in the
              loving hands of the Father.*

KEYWORD       *Going to be handed over.*

❧

**29**  A baptised person is a welcoming
person because baptism celebrates
welcome, God's welcome for us, our
welcome for one another. Parents

baptise their children with welcome in everyday caring. When we lift a hand to help, say a word to comfort or give joy we baptise the world.          cf Mt 21,28-32

PRAYER          *Lord, you encourage us to be sincere when we say yes to life. May our 'yes' be tasty with welcome, rather than empty with words.*

KEYWORD          *I will not go – but afterwards he went.*

**30**          Mary hates going back to work after illness. She has been demoted by the new takeover ownership. No longer her own phone, room or key. The great St Thérèse of Lisieux shows that being made little can be transformed with the power of love. The least can be great with childlike trust in the Father.
          cf Lk 9,46-50

PRAYER          *Lord, you encourage us with the life of St Thérèse of Lisieux. You show us that small is beautiful when touched with love like a little flower, a rose petal. Thérèse is happy to be a broom, to be used, but never used up.*

KEYWORD          *The least is great.*

*October*

**1**   The press was critical of the football tactics. St Paul says, "play meaning to win". Having to win at all costs can be calling down fire on my opponent. This merits strict rebuke from the Lord to his leaders.                            cf Lk 9,51-56

PRAYER   *Lord, help us to cope with rejection, with the one I think is the enemy. You remind us that it is the gentle that are strong. Blessed are the gentle.*

KEYWORD   *They went off to another village.*

❧

**2**   David fasted and prayed that God would leave him his love-child. When the news of the child's death came, David rose up, bathed and perfumed, dressed in kingly robes and made a feast. "Now is for living", he said, "my child will not come back to me, but I shall go to him."          cf Lk 9,57-62

PRAYER   *Lord, help us to leave our dead to your care, to let go the past to you. You promised to be with us in the 'now' of life, through this darkness, disappointment, pain and loss.*

KEYWORD   *Let the dead bury the dead.*

❧

**3**   The loving person does lovable things.
The peaceful person has peaceful ways.
Qualifying in God's kingdom is more
about attitude of heart, than logic of
mind. Talking to God, more than talking about God.                    cf Lk 10,1-12

PRAYER   *Lord, labourers of love live around us in
everyday family life, feeding, encouraging,
tolerating, being fair, showing ways of good
behaviour, developing character, focusing on
the wonder and mystery of God, caring for
the environment.*

KEYWORD   *Labourers to his harvest.*

**4**   The stable of Bethlehem welcomes all.
Rejection is our word, not God's. Hell is
God's love rejected by us, which is
mysterious beyond understanding.
                                  cf Lk 10,10-16

PRAYER   *Lord, it was you who created my being,
knit me together in my mother's womb.
I thank you for the wonder of my being,
for the wonder of all your creation.*

KEYWORD   *All mankind to see salvation.*

# 5

I got a surprise letter yesterday. It was full of praise for the efforts of a young parish which was trying to relate the sacraments to the lives of children, growing adults, and newly-weds.

cf Lk 10,17-24

PRAYER
*Lord, everything is entrusted to us by you. Help us to focus on your goodness rather than on our achievements.*

KEYWORD
*Hiding from the clever. Revealing to mere children.*

# 6

Is God on the landlord's side or on the tenants' side? He does not judge or punish, but challenges both to make this world a better world – to live, by being grown-up, playing fair.

cf Mt 21,33-43

PRAYER
*Lord, being grown-up helps us to respect the feelings of others, not to exploit them. Being grown-up means to excercise control over desires for drink, smoking and friendships. It means that I don't depend on the approval or applause of others for doing right or feeling good.*

KEYWORD
*The kingdom of God bears fruit.*

**7** There are three loves. Love of God, neighbour, and self. Our journey begins with love of self. If we don't love self we cannot love the neighbour. If we don't love the neighbour we cannot love God. Love of self is born in the home, from parents primarily. We cannot be loved too much.                    cf Lk 10,25-37

PRAYER   *Lord, bless parents in their sublime mission of helping children to feel appreciated, to know that they are precious and of value, priceless. This education makes for a healthy self-love.*

KEYWORD   *Who is my neighbour?*

**8** Conleth, the monk, met a spider. "Hello, Mr Spider", he said. "You are very beautiful." The monk lives in harmony with God, self and nature. Everything that exists is a voice of God. We are active persons, but also contemplative and reflective humans. Both are good. Martha and Mary are the same person: You and I.                    cf Lk 10,38-42

PRAYER   *Lord, it is true we don't have time to think, with the demands of family, work and business. In your graciousness you give us little moments of recreation, like making a flower arrangement, feeling the angelic beauty of babies and little children, counting a spider's legs, strolling with sea shells, watching a little boy learning to play football, a girl's hand and finger movement with a violin. "I have made all this for you", God says.*

KEYWORD       *Mary's part will not be taken from her.*

❧

**9**  Prayer is giving attention to the Father – God, and attention to the 'our' – all his people. Prayer that doesn't touch our attitudes to others is out of focus.

cf Lk 11,1-4

PRAYER       *Lord, you help us to give attention to you, in our private moments, in reading, in nature, in art, in music, in friendships. When we gather to pray in church you privilege us. You save us from excessive preoccupation with ourselves.*

KEYWORD       *Say our Father.*

❧

**10**  Etty Hilsum volunteered to go on the death train to Auschwitz. She wanted to be with her poor, frightened, broken people in the concentration camp. She

says, she can only pray for others, for
their well-being, and somehow, that
prayer lends them her strength and
spirit through God.        cf Lk 11,5-13

PRAYER        *Lord, help us in our prayers to get through
              the challenges of life rather than always
              wanting to win. May we trust your goodwill
              that always does what is best for us despite
              appearances and results.*

KEYWORD       *Ask and you will receive.*

**11**   She talked about the scourge of depres-
         sion. She thought that teaching little
         ones to express thanks from their earli-
         est years, was a healthy safeguard. It
         offset excessive, introvert, self-preoccu-
         pation. The emptiness in our spirit
         needs good company.        cf Lk 11,15-20

PRAYER        *Lord, an empty house with a 'For Sale' sign
              can invite trouble. Give us good company on
              our journey, like gratitude for you, thought
              for the neighbour and stranger. Joy for
              nature's exhibitions, courage to be first to
              forgive.*

KEYWORD       *An empty house – trouble.*

## 12

A voice from the crowd called out: May God Bless the mother that reared you. Yes, and bless those who help to rear others. He mentioned parents, neighbours, friends, grandparents, babysitters, teachers, those who help youth, carers for the sick, the smile of hospitality.

cf Lk 11,27-28

PRAYER

*Lord, Blessed Edmund Rice, although married and monied, gave his life and energy to reclaim the humanity of the poor peasants and under-privileged. He made education possible so that people could lift themselves out of the slums of depression and oppression.*

KEYWORD

*My brothers and sisters.*

## 13

Jesus paints a picture of God the Father as a crazy lover. He not only invites his unworthy children to the wedding feast of life, but marries into our family. He wants to share our kind of living, not as judge to exclude anyone, but as lover to embrace all.

cf Mt 22,1-14

PRAYER

*Lord, you accept the good and the bad in the human person. It was you who knit me together in my mother's womb. I thank you for the wonder of my being.*

KEYWORD

*Bring in good and bad, fill the banquet hall.*

**14** The witty man said, "They went and made a sin out of sex, and it is the most beautiful of God's blessings." Like Jonah we make God into a kind of oppressive tyrant, joyless, only watching for our sins. Jesus battles with this blindness. He calls us to a religion that's about life, growing-up, enthusiasm, laughter and wonder.                              cf Lk 11,29-32

PRAYER    *Lord, we even twist your word 'Repent' which is a call to look at life in a different way; a call to see wonder, beauty, goodness; to turn around; not to get bogged down in doom and gloom, in darkness, restrictions, devils and begrudging attitudes. A sign of Jonah is a footprint of the God of life.*

KEYWORD    *The Jonah sign is mercy.*

⁓

**15** Get the inside right, Jesus says. That's our thoughts, our perception, our way of seeing life. Otherwise our outside action can play false, and sound hollow. A test of our sincerity and integrity is if we do what we say. Hospitality to another is a good direction-finder.                              cf Lk 11,37-41

PRAYER    *Lord, bless those who give hospitality and kindness. We don't ask if they go to church.*

*We know that they have a truly godlike religion, of faith working through love.*

KEYWORD        *Your inward part – full of greed.*

**16**        When we point a finger of accusation at another, do we notice that the other three fingers point back at ourselves?

cf Lk 11,42-46

PRAYER        *Lord, why do we let small things annoy us and little worries upset us? We complain about the socks we wear until we see a person with no foot. Give us peace of mind that is not over-anxious, but anxious to be grateful and trusting.*

KEYWORD        *Finger to lift.*

**17**        The greatness of children is that they don't cover up truth. They are as they are, not worried about power, or what people think. They wonder at the things of life and love the joy of parties.

cf Lk 11,47-54.

PRAYER        *Lord, you long to see us childlike, then your spirit can give us peace and joy.*

KEYWORD        *"The wisdom of God".*

## 18

Thousands wanted to hear. He spoke about the apparent success of hypocrisy and evil. He said that God has the all-caring eye. Addressing fear of death, he said that God is greater than death. Even casual sparrows or lost hairs are not forgotten in God's love.          cf Lk 12,1-7

PRAYER

*Lord, without the sun, there would be no dancing shadows, and without the dark we would not see the stars. Help us to be trusting.*

KEYWORD

*Not one is forgotten with God.*

## 19

A good anything, including a good sermon, depends on the Holy Spirit. The Spirit is active when we have something to say, rather than saying something; when we speak what we feel, rather than what we think we should say.                      cf Lk 12,8-12.

PRAYER

*Lord, you give us two ears and one mouth. Should we try to listen twice as often as we talk?*

KEYWORD

*The Holy Spirit will teach you what I say.*

## 20

When we feel 'in bits' it is an arm of comfort, a hug of affection, a word of affirmation that gathers us together. God says he is the One who gathers us together; all our stray bits, odds and ends, successes and failures.

cf Jn 12,31-36

PRAYER    *Lord, bless all people in their responsibilities and missionaries who gather together broken and deprived people. They give human dignity to others through education and love, so that people can take themselves out of the slums of hopelessness.*

KEYWORD    *Gather the scattered.*

## 21

Midas turned everything into gold. When a greedy man had his daughter turned into gold he was broken-hearted. Now he missed her smile, her voice, her affection, her presence. He had exchanged life for a shiny lifeless thing.

cf Lk 12,13-21

PRAYER    *Lord, we thank you for the gift of life. Help us not to be over-anxious with owning shiny things. Give us the balance of generous hearts and hands.*

KEYWORD    *Life not secure by owning things.*

**22** All life is waiting. We wait to be born. We wait to die. We wait for the dawn. We wait to grow. We wait for one another. We can make waiting a blessing through attentiveness. Jesus says, have an eye for the other person.

cf Lk 12,35-38

PRAYER    *Lord, a great artist said he did not have to leave his own room or window to be creative. He found peace in attentiveness to small things in the ordinary surrounds of his life, looking at spiders. This is your way. May it be our way.*

KEYWORD   *Be waiting.*

**23** Taking responsibility is the making of a person. The wise parent encourages responsibility in children. In our make-up the jawbone talks a lot. The knuckle-bone objects to everything; the wish-bone dreams and fantasies; but it's the backbone that takes on responsibility for others.          cf Lk 12,39-48

PRAYER    *Lord, bless parents and leaders in the world of responsibility. Encourage us to be responsible in little ways, keeping a promise, turning up on time, taking the dog for a walk, making our environment litter-free.*

KEYWORD   *Stand ready.*

## 24

I am half-mystic, half-nut; my eyes upon the stars, my feet in the mud. One moment I am kind and big-hearted, the next sneaky and cruel. It's weird how a person can be split like that, part God, part scallywag.                    cf Lk 12,49-53

PRAYER    *Lord, now I know that flawed lives are good. Through my weaknesses I possess the key to every heart that is sad, shamed or soiled, so I am glad you made me as I am – philosopher and fool.*

KEYWORD   *Peace and distress.*

## 25

Make friends. Give love. Make no ene-mies. That was his mother's advice. We make decisions about what we wear, what we eat, how, when and where we recreate. Making decisions about what is right brings harmony of spirit and gives peace of mind.                    cf Lk 12,54-59

PRAYER    *Lord, I admired her decision. She gave up her planned date and night out when a neighbour-friend called unexpectedly to have her sick child taken to hospital.*

KEYWORD   *Judge what is right.*

## 26

A mother reflecting on her newborn said that goodness is not so much a state of being as an openness to change and to learning. There is the muck and luck, the hours of waiting, getting it wrong. There are no quick fixes, miracles or revelations in the mission of rearing children.                    cf Lk 13,1-9

PRAYER      *Lord, you do not take away our bundle of difficulties, the feeling of getting nowhere, recycling the same old temptations. Do give us an attitude of humble acceptance of our lives, and the fig tree manure we find in ourselves. Strengthen our trust that nothing can take your love from us.*

KEYWORD     *Manure it.*

❧

## 27

Millennium predictions about the end of the world distract us from God's real message – that we care for one another and make our world a better place now. We cannot see or touch God, but we can see and touch a neighbour, a stranger, a child, a lonely person, a friend.

cf Mt 22,34-40

PRAYER      *Lord, love of neighbour and love of self give us a balance in loving you. Too much God and no neighbour is not the Jesus of the*

*Good Samaritan and too much neighbour*
*and no God is not the Jesus who gives*
*thanks to the Father for all.*

KEYWORD          *Love your neighbour as yourself.*

❧

## 28

There is a difference between religious practice and spirituality. People often don't understand church services or Mass. They do understand the everyday needs of little children and people, giving a hand to help out, respecting the feelings of others, caring for the environment.                    cf Lk 13,10-17

PRAYER          *Lord, everyday life is not lived in church or chapel but in homes, in work, on the road. The Church calls us together to express gratitude. This is an invitation from God to encourage and nourish us to be human.*

KEYWORD          *Untie her bonds on the sabbath day.*

❧

## 29

When things are thrown at us unexpectedly, we are stressed. Life has an odd mix of good and bad, in ourselves and in others. The kingdom of God is hidden in the mix and mess of seeds thrown into the unknown, producing extraordinarily results.          cf Lk 13,18-21

PRAYER · *Lord, we like to control life, make our own achievements. Yet nothing is our achievement, all is your goodness. Maybe we can only learn that message through weakness, powerlessness and dependency.*

KEYWORD · *A mustard seed thrown into a garden.*

**30** A little boy put his hand into the sweet jar. He grabbed a big handful of sweets. Then he couldn't extract his hand from the jar. It had got too fat. He was imprisoned. If he took less he'd be free.

cf Lk 13,20-30

PRAYER · *Lord, because we are precious to you, you encourage us not to be grabbing and greedy. Carrying too much baggage and forgetting others is not good for our human spirit.*

KEYWORD · *Enter by a narrow gate.*

**31** The accommodation was bad. People were different. It was lonely. Nobody seemed to care. The temptation was to pack up and leave. Years later, looking back, that experience of staying, through the cloudy days, gives great joy. We cannot separate the messiness of Good Friday from the joy at Easter time.

cf Lk 13,31-35

PRAYER

*Lord, in our decisions to leave, to come and go, you give us great freedom. Often we don't know what is best. You stayed through Jerusalem, thinking of us when it was difficult.*

KEYWORD

*I must go on in Jerusalem.*

# November

**1**

A little boy asked, "Who are the people in the coloured windows of the church?" "They are the saints", replied his dad. "What are the saints?" he inquired. After a pause the little boy said, "I know". Saints are people who let the light shine through them.

cf Lk 14,1-6

**PRAYER**

*Lord, I saw your light shine through yesterday at the hospital – Mary at her husband's sick bedside day and night; her husband raising a smile of gratitude; a friend who bought me a lotto ticket for a surprise; the people I always see minding children; those who help and organize football games; people who remember birthday parties and anniversaries. All are lights of goodness. Most pass unrecorded, hidden and unnoticed. We need a thanksgiving day for all the unsung saints of everyday living.*

**KEYWORD**

*Curing on the Sabbath.*

～

**2**

The vocations director asked the young man, "Are you weak enough to take on being a priest?" We depend, for survival. We are not self-made. Can we acknowledge our longing, and need for affection, our inadequacy to cope? Have we a trust in God that helps us through our limitations – putting our hand in his?

cf Lk 14,1-11

PRAYER     *Lord, it is the affection of people, the
           friendliness of children that keeps us going.
           To be humble means to recognise our
           earthiness '(humus)'. Among our earthiest
           words, the angels stray.*

KEYWORD    *Humble to exalt.*

                                        ❧

**3**    I saw the accident. A van crossing the
         main road did not see an oncoming car.
         The car driver was trapped by the im-
         pact. I was tempted to pass by and leave
         it to others. A similar personal experi-
         ence some months ago made me wish
         that someone would get involved, take a
         risk. I gave my name and address to the
         man in the car.                  cf Mt 23,1-12

PRAYER   *Lord, it is good when fear goes out of
         religion; but love must go into living, love
         that parents understand, like giving time to
         others, taking risks, getting involved,
         respecting feelings. There is more to life
         than church-going. Yet, church warms us
         into loving.*

KEYWORD  *Not lifting a finger.*

                                        ❧

**4**    I always find joy, welcome and hospital-
         ity in St Joseph's. It is a house that cares
         for the mentally handicapped among

the elderly. The capacity for goodness
among the poor, the crippled, the lame
and the blind is celebrated.

cf Lk 14,1-11

PRAYER        *Lord, the way we celebrate our weak and
              powerless is a measure of our humanity,
              and a reminder of your goodness.*

KEYWORD       *Invite the poor, crippled, lame and blind.*

⁓

5    We are the poor, because we die, and are
     dependent. We are the crippled because
     of the handicaps that life serves through
     marriage, family, friendship and busi-
     ness. We are the blind because we
     cannot see the good in others who think
     differently to us, nor the good in our-
     selves. We are the lame because we
     cannot keep pace with what others
     expect of us. But we are the people
     invited to God's banquet. cf Lk 14,15-24

PRAYER        *Lord, for some mysterious reason you love
              the mix of our humanity. You married into
              us. You know us inside out. You call us your
              delight.*

KEYWORD       *Bring in the poor, crippled, blind and lame
              – sinners.*

⁓

**6**     Jesus knows his audience – fathers, mothers, wives, children, brothers, sisters, builders, war-makers. His advice is you can take nothing with you out of this life, except a good heart, kind spirit, joy, hospitality. So start practising them now.                    cf Lk 14,25-33

PRAYER     *Lord, thank you for the blessings of life. Help us to balance our wants with our needs. Give us this day our daily bread.*

KEYWORD     *Possessions.*

❧

**7**     Only a doting shepherd would leave ninety-nine good sheep in danger in the wilderness and go searching for the stray one. The God of Jesus Christ is a lover of strays. He never gives up his search for us. He never closes the door on frail humanity.                    cf Lk 15,1-10

PRAYER     *Lord, you show your respect for the ninety-nine in the way you treat the one with extravagant and abundant generosity. We may leave our Father's house but our Father never leaves us.*

KEYWORD     *The missing one.*

❧

## 8

No matter how saucy or terrible the story, my friend always commented: "Isn't that very interesting now." Jesus did not let himself get pushed into judgemental condemnations. A man gets the sack for irresponsibility. He organizes 'a fiddle' with the customers for the rainy day. What do you think of that? Great imagination!     cf Lk 16,1-8

PRAYER      *Lord, you advise us to be careful about weeds in our make-up, not to be too hasty in rooting them up. Better to wait, be patient, because the weeds of failure today can be the flower of tomorrow's goodness.*

KEYWORD     *Praising astuteness.*

## 9

The Pharisees loved money. So do we. Money is a basic necessity. Jesus says, "let it be a servant of blessing rather than a master of greed".     cf Lk 16,9-15

PRAYER      *Lord, is our excessive love of money a substitute for real love missed out, a basic insecurity? Help us to trust our Father who gives all and to share our blessings with one another.*

KEYWORD     *Use money.*

**10** We grow tired waiting – waiting for healing, waiting for the exam, for the job, for the doctor's report, queuing for a living, wondering about Mister or Miss Right. This is the human condition. Because God is our hidden God, always with us, our waiting need not be boring.

cf Mt 25,1-13

PRAYER    *Lord, you give us an awesome capacity to better life, to make good, to use imagination, to raise a laugh. Three school boys on three stray horses led a merry dance through peak hour city traffic last week. The rumbling business world all stood still for some minutes. The magic of the horse, the joyful imagination of the youngsters grabbed my attention. They were quickly sidelined by the law.*

KEYWORD   *Stay awake.*

**11** The child's mother died. The father had difficulty coping. There was goodwill, but a lot of emotional insecurity. Damage done carried over into the child's own marriage. There is over-anxiety about money. There is excessive longing for someone to make one happy, when reality says one can only make oneself happy.

cf Lk 17,1-6

PRAYER    *Lord, help me to see the obstacles in my*
          *make-up that cause hurt to others, because*
          *of damage in my own past. It is the loving*
          *decisions made now that make life, not*
          *hangovers from the past.*

KEYWORD   *Obstacles come but don't make them.*

∽

**12** Writing helps to express something
       inside oneself. The something is bor-
       rowed or programmed from somewhere
       else. St Francis said it well: "Make me a
       channel of your peace."        cf Lk 17,7-10

PRAYER    *Lord, the original, the origin, the source of*
          *all is you – God our Friend, with three*
          *names: Father, Son and Spirit.*

KEYWORD   *We are servants, receivers.*

∽

**13** Mary is destroying herself with envy,
       jealousy and hatred for her ex-partner.
       She lights candles to get him back. Our
       cure is not always in getting what we
       want, but asking if there is another way.
                                        cf Lk 17,11-19

PRAYER    *Lord, it is our attitude in life that needs*
          *your help and healing. Only one of the ten*

*healed had the right attitude of openness to change and gratitude for what is.*

KEYWORD      *Where are the other nine?*

**14**   Bring back the old ways. Fill the churches. The religious leaders have let us down. I heard him on the radio. Yet Jesus said, "I must suffer grievously and be rejected." The full story of a tree isn't in its leaves. They fall away and die. But there is inner beauty. There is life in its nakedness. There is 'a spirituality' even when the leaves of people in churches cannot be seen, because God says, "I am with you always."          cf Lk 17,20-25

PRAYER     *Lord, open my eyes and deepen my trust to see your presence and Kingdom, not in places but in people of all shades and religions and differences, in anybody who desires to help, to better our world, to share resources, to plead for human rights and suffer for peace and justice.*

KEYWORD     *Kingdom is among you.*

## 15

The ads say, 'use me, take me, eat me, smell me, drink me, bank with me'. They all want my body. I sure am somebody. Is there more to me? What's my body for? What is a recipe for happiness?

cf Lk 17,26-31

PRAYER

*Lord, you tell us that our bodies are not made for vultures. They are in your image, for a loving relationship. Through our bodies we express love. Love is our calling. Love is our fulfilment in Heaven. No body – no love.*

KEYWORD

*Not for vultures.*

## 16

Does God delay help to us, 'till justice is done'? The justice of God is respect for people. When people's traditions, differences, property, have been dis-respected, this truth has to be faced and spoken. Then comes reconciliation. It is we who delay God's help.     cf Lk 18,1-8

PRAYER

*Lord, there is a temptation to whitewash the hurts and injustices of the past – in fami-lies, among nations. Might and success have been made right, but also blind. Help us to face the enemy within us – go and be reconciled.*

KEYWORD

*See justice done.*

*17*   I met the First Communion children
with their teacher, in church, during
school time. I showed them what we
'do' at Sunday Mass – how we pray
together. Nourishing the Spirit helps the
total well-being of a child. Their spirit of
wonder, beauty, caring, gratitude, enthusiasm, is a joy to experience, and sad if
forgotten or not encouraged.

cf Mt 25,14-30

PRAYER   *Lord, I promised at baptism to care for the
total well-being of a child. Help us in this
awesome and wonderful responsibility. Send
your Spirit upon us to guide and direct our
ways.*

KEYWORD   *Our talent.*

~

*18*   Thomas Merton is a spiritual giant. He
reflects on human emotions. He says
that sexual temptation, envy, or anger
can often be brought into line not by
violent attack or repression, but by
making our life emotionally richer. An
opera, an art gallery, a walk in the
woods, a symphony may lift us out of
self-destructive tendencies.

cf Lk 18,35-43

PRAYER   *Lord, you invited the objectors to bring the
blind man to you for healing. You see our*

*capacity for goodness, when we ourselves
often see only weeds.*

KEYWORD        *Bring the man to him.*

❧

**19**   The freedom-from-anxiety prayer at
Mass means release from a twisted view
of life; from having a chip on the shoulder; anger with age, resentment of
others and the world.        cf Lk 19,1-10

PRAYER        *Lord, that I may see; to be mellow with life,
not bitter; to be open to delight, not begrudging; to admire success in others, not
jealous; to be honest about my weakness,
not passing the book of blame to others; to
be gentle, not harsh; to give the sign of
peace; to have freedom from anxiety.*

KEYWORD        *Anxious to see.*

❧

**20**   Playing the game of life is being ready
for the next pass rather than waiting for
the final whistle. The next pass is the
everyday call to care for family and
friend; to make a better world, to find
the secret for my own happiness.
                                cf Lk 19,12-27

PRAYER
*Lord, we can see and speak to one another, become friends, share our joys and sorrows. The real joy is in serving you.*

KEYWORD
*Do business until I get back.*

❧

**21** He loved his native city. He longed for its peace. Opportunity knocks. But we don't recognise new ideas, new ways forward, people's rights.

cf Lk 19,41-44

PRAYER
*Lord, I liked it when you cried over your native city. Cities nourish us with wonder, delights, and refreshing experiences. Their stones tell their history. To serve a city and its people is a way to peace.*

KEYWORD
*He saw the city and wept.*

❧

**22** His teaching was a breath of fresh air. God is not confined to temple or place. God roams where we are; strays among the weary and the sinful. Authority does not like the freedom of this good news.

cf Lk 19,45-48

PRAYER
*Lord, you are kind to us and to all people. For this we thank you. You will fill us with*

*the joy of your Spirit, that we may renew
the earth.*

**KEYWORD**     *Hung on his words.*

**23**    A contented woman was asked where
          she would like to be buried. She said, "I
          don't mind where, because God will
          find me wherever I am."

                                      cf Lk 20,27-40

**PRAYER**    *Lord, we cannot control most of what
              happens – how we were born, the weather,
              happenings in life. We can't even control
              the consequences of our own decisions. Help
              us to trust your loving providence.*

**KEYWORD**    *To God all are alive.*

**24**    Sabrina died tragically during the week.
          She was 19 years old. She was a run-
          away from home; expelled from school.
          A little girl told me that Sabrina gave her
          a Christmas present every year. The
          child's evaluation of Sabrina's life
          reminds me that God only knows how
          to love, never to be angry, only to wel-
          come, never to condemn.

                                      cf Mt 25,31-46

PRAYER    *Lord, because God is love, we are always called to be loving people. It is an exciting challenge and vocation. God helps us in all kinds of ways if we want to be loving.*

KEYWORD   *God loves – it is we who curse.*

&#x223D;

**25**     A man in love living in a slum is happier than a loveless millionaire living in a mansion. A man picking up litter and leaves in the park was whistling during his labour of love. Most of us forget to say thanks to church or family. But if we do the right thing with love, happiness happens.

cf Lk 21,1-4

PRAYER    *Lord, doing the 'right thing' is peacemaking. Doing 'things right' can be a show-off, a passing exhibition that glistens but hasn't enduring qualities of character and integrity.*

KEYWORD   *The widow's coin.*

&#x223D;

**26**     The mother explained that the birth of a child is not neat or orderly, but more of blood and guts. Beauty and joy are mixed with pain and poverty. She

concludes that we must be loved greatly
in our imperfect ways, because such is
our world.                        cf Lk 21,5-12

PRAYER        *Lord, in your providence we emerge from
              one womb and are embraced in a second
              womb which is beyond our understanding.
              We call this your loving kindness and
              mercy.*

KEYWORD       *Fearful sights and great signs from heaven.*

❧

**27**  Bad things happened to Etty Hilsum.
        She chose to die with her people in a
        concentration camp in Auschwitz. Her
        diaries were found. Her thoughts are
        most inspiring to read. God hides in
        darkness.                        cf Lk 21,12-19

PRAYER        *Lord, bad things happen. Sometimes we can
              blame ourselves. Other times it's out of our
              control. We don't know the why. But we do
              know that when bad things happen you are
              always present. Hidden in death is resurrec-
              tion.*

KEYWORD       *Hated, but not a hair lost.*

❧

# 28

A child learning to walk breaks down
often and breaks up a lot. It is the price
to pay for new found freedom and
liberation.                              cf Lk 21,20-28

PRAYER        *Lord, the world is forever learning to walk;
              breaking down and breaking up. You
              promised to gather our scattered stray selves
              in your Kingdom.*

KEYWORD       *Stand erect – Liberation is at hand.*

# 29

I like Sister Ruth Burrow's ideas. We live
with inconsistency all the time, in
ourselves, in our changing world. The
only consistency (security) is the word
of God, that says, "we are loved without
condition, not because of anything we
do, or merit, but because God is good."
All is given free. We are simply receivers.
                                         cf Lk 21,29-33

PRAYER        *Lord, poems are made by fools like me, but
              only God can make a tree, a tree that
              receives all from earth and mother nature,
              and in receiving gives glory to the world.*

KEYWORD       *Think of the fig tree.*

**30** There is public life, private life, and inner soul life. We are encouraged to be awake to our capacity to give gratitude, awake from taking so much for granted, awake to nature's daily exhibition, awake to noticing the gift of others with praise.                                              cf Lk 21,34-36

PRAYER     *Lord, the heart is a mirror of my life. But that mirror is lost in the greater mirror of your unconditional love.*

KEYWORD    *Stand with confidence.*

# December

*1*

Why did you let us stray, and get our-selves in a mess? Why didn't you shock us into loving ways? "Because my love is different", God says. You may leave the Father's house, but the Father never leaves you, sinner or saint. He even hides his face in kindness. Are we awake to this good news?

cf Is 63,16-17.64,1-8

PRAYER

*Lord, you call us your clay, not even your pot or your glass or silver show-piece. But, with a touch of the master's hand clay has infinite possibilities. Be alert – we are all the work of your hand.*

KEYWORD

*And yet Lord you are our Father.*

*2*

All kinds of circumstances prevent us from being with people in person, during times of pain or joy. But we can always say a word – say a silent prayer, have a heart-wish and it counts. The written word can be a powerful healer.

cf Mt 8,5-11

PRAYER

*Lord, recently among my souvenirs I found a letter. It was full of compliments, and affectionately written to me years ago. Re-reading the letter gave me encouragement. I phoned the writer to say thanks.*

KEYWORD

*Say but the word.*

# 3

We long to be accepted, in all our weakness and vulnerability, despite the hidden skeletons in our human cupboard. Jesus knows that the Father accepts us totally, as we are, like little children. He is filled with joy. He longs to share that joy with us.   cf Lk 10,21-24

PRAYER

*Lord, as a child I remember knocking off apples in our neighbour's orchard. Years later that neighbour told me that he used to see me, but pretended that he did not, lest I'd be embarrassed or get hurt. You too hide your face in kindness.*

KEYWORD

*Fill with joy.*

# 4

I wondered why Jesus sat there in the hills when he could have gone to the lame, the blind and the crippled, saving them trouble. Do we evaluate ourselves too often by what we do, our activity? A baby cannot prove itself nor can a person who is severely mentally ill or badly handicapped. Yet they are precious. With God we are simply loved whether we sit, sleep, do or don't.
                                    cf Mt 15,29-37

PRAYER

*Lord, I wonder what way the lame, crippled and blind were healed. Were they made to feel good about themselves for the first time*

*ever in the presence of this man? Bless
people who make us feel good.*

KEYWORD *He sat there in the hills.*

∽

5

It is said that prayer that doesn't disturb
the heart is no prayer. Because God is
love our relationship with love has to
warm us into practical loving of God's
family, and indeed of all his creation.
cf Mt 7,21-24.27

PRAYER *Lord, wherever, whenever, or however
people are helped God is praised and
Christmas is happening.*

KEYWORD *Listening and acting.*

∽

6

Loneliness touches all our lives. If our
response to the interruptions and frus-
trations of living, is a desire to reach
deeper appreciation, with compassion
and hospitality, then loneliness converts
into peace of mind and solitude. This is
the thinking of the writer, Henry Nou-
wen. cf Mt 9,27-37

PRAYER *Lord, when you gave people their sight, I
wonder did their happiness increase. Did
they get a new insight into the ordinary*

*things in life? Did they grow in apprecia-*
*tion and gratitude? You promise us your*
*spirit of insight.*

KEYWORD          *Two blind men followed.*

❧

7   We'll miss Grandpa at Christmas. His
    presence meant so much, and it was
    unnoticed, cooling down arguments in
    the family, talking with the children,
    telling stories, giving bits of advice. He
    was a healer, a raiser of spirits, an advis-
    er. He blessed all with his power of
    goodness.                    cf Mt 9,35.10,11.18

PRAYER           *Lord, you give us power to raise another's*
                 *spirit, to give a laugh or smile, to speak a*
                 *compassionate word over human weakness*
                 *and tragedy. Our hands are in the hands of*
                 *the One who stills the waters.*

KEYWORD          *Hidden goodness.*

❧

8   It is a special birthday today. The church
    and font of my baptism in Ferbane is
    one hundred years old. Famine people
    that I never saw or met gave me this gift.
    I, in turn, was privileged to build a
    church and font because of them. The

beautiful spire is memory to their love
and sacrifice. It never fails to inspire.

cf Mk 1,1-8

PRAYER     *Lord, bless those who have gone before us.*
*Most of our everyday efforts like Christmas*
*shopping, cooking, visiting, remembering,*
*collecting are never registered, and often*
*unnoticed. But all is scraped into the heart*
*of God. All counts and is not forgotten.*

KEYWORD    *Voices preparing the way.*

**9**   The Christian good news is that we
don't have to buy, merit or earn God's
mercy and forgiveness. Jesus does not
say, 'I forgive'. He knows the Father
always forgives.          cf Lk 5,17-26

PRAYER     *Lord, the fact that we are always forgiven is*
*not an excuse to condone sin or to go soft on*
*goodness, but rather a reason to trust*
*ourselves as we are, into the arms of mercy*
*and let God's word heal us.*

KEYWORD    *Your sins are forgiven.*

**10** They picked him up as a stray. He is full of affection and personality. He keeps Carmel company everyday in her wheelchair. He delights visitors with his tricks. He is full of fun. He strays a lot, but is always drawn back home. He is a favourite dog.

cf Mt 18,12-14

PRAYER *Lord, you love strays. Is it that wild human streak in us that always draws us back to you? Because you can never let any of your little ones be lost.*

KEYWORD *Stray, not lost.*

**11** Jesus harnessed himself to the yoke of our humanity. He has blessed the stresses and strains, the weakness and imperfection of our daily existence.

cf Mt 11,28-30

PRAYER *Lord, it is true we can never get anything totally right, nor do we even know the honesty of our own intentions, nor can we be perfectly sure. We are inconsistent. Yet you love us the way we are.*

KEYWORD *Come to me, overburdened.*

## 12

John, rough and ready, was not afraid to face the injustice of Salome. Elijah was not afraid to take on Jezebel. Jesus is the new Elijah, not afraid to take on the injustice of the world and redeem both the victims and the victimisers.

cf Mt 11,11-15

PRAYER

*Lord, you came down to earth. Help us to be down-to-earth people in the way that we treat one another.*

KEYWORD

*The least is great.*

## 13

Gluttons, drunkards, prostitutes, tax collectors, were friends of Jesus. I wonder why. He must have spoken their language. To be accepted he must have enjoyed their company. He did not moralise at them.          cf Mt 11,16-19

PRAYER

*Lord, thank you for loving me. I'm sorry for not loving others, and not loving you. Help me to live like Jesus.*

KEYWORD

*Look, a glutton and a drunkard.*

**14** King Ahab envied Naboath's little garden. Jezebel, the king's wife organised the murder of Naboath, so that the garden would be his and hers. Elijah shouts everywhere, 'foul play, foul play'. Elijah takes on Jezebel, but he has to flee for his life.                cf Mt 17,10-13

PRAYER    *Lord, you are the new Elijah, pleading justice and fair play for all people. Bless those who work and suffer for human rights, for the true freedom of peoples, who make paths of peace.*

KEYWORD   *Justice.*

**15** John wasn't sure about Jesus. Life is not meant to be totally clear. There are no complete answers. The visitors didn't see the lame, blind, crippled and deaf being cured. Did they want to see? Do we?
                cf Jn 1,6-8.19.28

PRAYER    *Lord, because you are love, the way of knowing seems to be through the heart experience, waiting and longing, not just learning facts.*

KEYWORD   *I am not the Christ.*

**16** Jesus clashes with authority when it wears a hard face or is insensitive to the poor, and wants to control everybody. There is only one author – source of goodness – that is God.    cf Mt 21,23-27

PRAYER     *Lord, thank you for using authority to empty yourself with goodness and blessing for our world.*

KEYWORD    *Authority.*

**17** Nobody is rejected at Bethlehem. Jesus says that prostitutes and detested tax collectors are God's chosen children. Religion can be an obstacle, when we think that we earn or deserve God's love. His goodness is without condition.
                              cf Mt 21,28-32

PRAYER     *Lord, we are nothing without you. You sustain us with your mercy.*

KEYWORD    *Tax collectors and prostitutes.*

**18** Emmanuel means, God is with us; not just at special times, or in special places, but in the flesh of our humanity, with all its roguish adventures.

cf Mt 1,18-24

PRAYER *Lord, the priest was right when he prayed, "The Lord is with you." But we need help to see, and see, again and again.*

KEYWORD *Emmanuel – God is with us.*

❧

**19** She spoke critical unfair words to the father of two children in the pub. The children were behaving irresponsibly and distracting everybody. The father replied, "You are right, I am inadequate. I have come from the hospital where their young mother has just died." Our vision is often limited.     cf Lk 1,5-25

PRAYER *Lord, if we haven't something good to say, help us to be silent, until our vision grows. We never know the full story of the other. We cannot even know ourselves.*

KEYWORD *How can I be sure?*

❧

## 20

Come Lord Jesus. Come and be born in our hearts. There are different kinds of birth: Mary, Elizabeth, me. Joan was the lowest paid, with a happy disposition. She gives a little gift to everyone at work at Christmas time. Her adult friends are jealous. They try to demean her.

PRAYER

*Lord, bring to birth love when there is jealousy in me, compassion when criticism is harsh, openness of mind when I am begrudging, with a chip on my shoulder. Bring humour and tolerance when I am tempted to be resentful and sour.*

KEYWORD

*Barren, the spirit will come.*

## 21

Christmas is God turning up in unexpected ways, in odd places, an unusual birth – Mary, a surprise pregnancy – Elizabeth. The pub, the shop, the beach, the park, watching and waiting, singing, God hidden in sinners and saints.

cf Lk 1,39-45

PRAYER

*Lord, Mary got in touch with Elizabeth celebrating the first Christmas. Getting in touch with each other is at the heart of celebrating Christmas.*

KEYWORD

*Sinners and saints blessing the world.*

**22**  We get disturbed with unexpected news, sudden illness or death, a lost job, an unplanned pregnancy, a misunderstanding, quickening age, the same old temptations. We are gripped with spasms of fear. We need God's healing words, "Don't be afraid, I am with you, you are my favourite."          cf Lk 1,26-38

PRAYER  *Lord, you were with David in all his expeditions. Give me encouragement as I struggle through mine.*

KEYWORD  *Deeply disturbed.*

**23**  Elizabeth's baby is a bundle of promise, destined for mystery. We have the same credentials. We are right to celebrate birth with wonder and excitement, and ponder over our name.          cf Lk 1,57-66

PRAYER  *Lord, help us to celebrate our children, and to celebrate too 'the child' in ourselves, that longs for wonder, excitement, delight, despite our second-hand wrapping that annoys us sometimes.*

KEYWORD  *The name is.*

**24** Tender mercy is God's name, Zachariah says, "and it is not 'knowledge' of sins, that catches his mercy, but it is forgiveness of sin".                    cf Lk 1,67-79

PRAYER     *Lord, give me the understanding I need to accept myself with peace, my family and different peoples.*

KEYWORD    *Tender mercy.*

**25** A little child looking into the crib called the names, "There's the Baby Jesus, that's Mary his mammy, and the other man, and the newcomers are the three wild men". Wild humanity is blessed forever.                    cf Lk 2,1-14

PRAYER     *Lord, because of you the word became flesh. You bless our fleshiness. Help us to put flesh into our words as we walk the journey of life.*

KEYWORD    *Word made flesh.*

**26** We are not promised an easy road. But we are promised the assurance of God's love in our odd make-up. There is the constant prompting, "Don't be afraid".                    cf Mt 10,17-22

PRAYER   *Lord, help me to cope with fear, about myself, about family and the happenings of life. You have the whole world in your hands. Alleluia.*

KEYWORD   *Don't worry.*

❧

**27**   "Was she running away from something?" the hermit's father was asked about his daughter. "No, she is running towards something", he said. The hermit does not rationalise about God's existence. Her heart, like the poet, praises God's importance and sees the touch of the master's hand in all that exists.                          cf Jn 20,2-8

PRAYER   *Lord, Magdalene, Peter, and John ran because their hearts were full of good news that God, despite all the failures, misgivings and deathblows that we give ourselves, loves us into his family. We have reason to be enthusiastic people.*

KEYWORD   *Running.*

❧

**28**   Baby Moses escaped murder. He became a great leader and liberator. The child Jesus is the new Moses. He liberates us from the slavery of guilt, fear and mean-

ingless living. He accompanies us to our
new home.                      cf Mt 2,12-18

PRAYER       *Lord, at Christmas time familiar faces of
             our dear departed appear. Help us to think
             of death as a friend, that in your providence
             carries us into loving arms.*

KEYWORD      *Escape.*

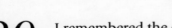

**29**       Every family is a holy family because
             family is God's idea. No family is perfect
             is also God's idea. We struggle with
             problems and troubles, our own inade-
             quacies, the other person's differences
             and weaknesses.            cf Lk 2,22-40

PRAYER       *Lord, there is goodness in the worst of us
             and evil in the best of us. Your mercy
             embraces all of us. Help us to live together
             with tolerance, compassion and humour.*

KEYWORD      *Growing up.*

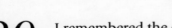

**30**       I remembered the child's disappoint-
             ment. He said, "You shook hands with
             me, but you never looked at me." God
             gives us total attention, in taking on our
             human condition. He always looks
             lovingly on each one of us – his chil-
             dren.                       cf Lk 2,36-40

PRAYER          *Lord, thank you for loving me. Help me to*
                *look lovingly on other people and to realise*
                *that* PRAYER *is letting you look at me.*

KEYWORD         *Look.*

**31**          Today, is "white and blue, green and
                red". The love of God, our Daily Bread.
                Love is given like the sun without
                condition. Love parcelled in the flesh of
                touches, the smiles of affection, the
                colours of nature, and the work of
                human hands.                    cf Jn 1,1-18

PRAYER          *Lord, teach us to value all the good you*
                *have given us which are foretastes of eternal*
                *life.*

**KEYWORD**     *Your love is eternal.*